R A W R

journal

12 week Food & Exercise Journal

#MandalaMadness

12 week Food & Exercise Journal: #MandalaMadness

First Printing 2017

RAWR World Pty Ltd

www.rawrworld.com

Name:

....

Phone No:

....

Date Started:

....

Date Finished:

....

... a note from the author ...

Congratulations on taking a step towards your goals,
dreams and most importantly ... results!!!
I created these journals because I wanted a quick and
easy system to keep myself in check when it came towards
my health goals. I am a huge fan of writing things down,
reviewing and creating bigger goals from that.
This journal creates pure focus so you can push
through any obstacles that may come your way.
I hope you enjoy using this journal as much as I love
creating it for you.

natalie x

Write down your gaols for each
week! Be sure to write down what
you want ... see what you can
come up with!

Goals:

Complete all my sessions // Drink 4 liters of water

....

....

....

Measurements:

Chest	Waist ....
Umbilicus	Hips ....
Right Bicep	Left Bicep ....
Right Thigh	Left Thigh ....
Right Calf	Left Calf ....

Record your
measurements.
They are a
more
accountable
way of
measuring
progress than
weighing
yourself.

Progress Picture: []

Remember to take a
progress picture
every week!

This weeks Inspiration:

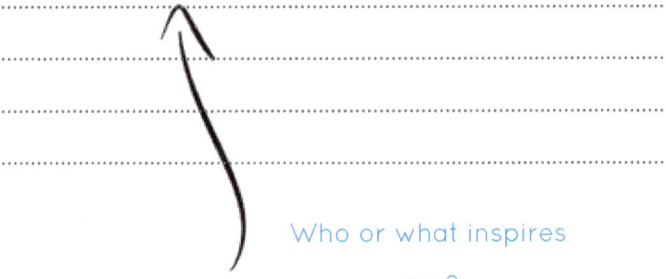

....

....

....

....

Who or what inspires
you?

the how to... part 1

. Training Schedule .

Monday:

am ....

pm ....

Tuesday:

am ...... 530 am - Gym - Legs ....

pm ....

Wednesday:

am ...... 530 am - boot camp ....

pm ....

Thursday:

am ....

pm ....

Friday:

am ....

pm ...... 630 pm - 5km jog ....

Saturday:

am ....

pm ....

Plan your sessions at the beginning of every week! How many sessions do you want to do and when do you want to do them?

Attitude of gratitude! Just writing 3
simple things that you are grateful /
appreciate in your life. It will set you
up every single day!

. A P P R E C I A T I O N .

1. Coffee with great friends.
2. ....
3. ....

! Be sure to write down
what you eat to keep
yourself accountable
to your goals. .

. F O O D .

Meal 1:
1 x toast with 2 x eggs
....
....calories: 360

W
E
E
K
•
1

Meal 2:
chicken and salad wrap
....
....calories: 470

Meal 3:
....
....calories: ....

M
T
W
T
F
S
S

Meal 4:
....
....calories: ....

Meal 5:
....
....calories: ....

Meal 6:
....
....calories: ....
....total calories: ....

Remember
to circle
what day it
is so you can
keep track
of where
you are.

the how to... part 1

The perfect spot to jot down all your resistance work!

.WEIGHT·TRAINING.

exercise	set 1	set 2	set 3	set 4	set 5	set 6
Squats	/ 12	/ 12	/	/	/	/
Push ups	/ 15	/ 15	/	/	/	/
	/	/	/	/	/	/
	/	/	/	/	/	/
	/	/	/	/	/	/
	/	/	/	/	/	/
	/	/	/	/	/	/

.AEROBIC.

activity	duration	distance	resistance	calories
Stair-master	45 mins	-	level 4	460

Whenever you do aerobic activity, be sure to write as much information as you can.

.RECOVERY/STRETCHES.

activity .... duration

All muscles used stretched // Glute mobility work // Foam roller for legs

Mobility and recovery work is very important! Be sure to stretch.

.WATER.

Be sure to drink your water every day! These cups can either be a cup of water or a liter of water.

Enjoy x

WEEK · 1

The most common way people give up their power is by thinking they don't have any.

Goals:

....

....

....

....

....

Measurements:

.... Chest   Waist ....

.... Umbilicus   Hips ....

.... Right Bicep   Left Bicep ....

.... Right Thigh   Left Thigh ....

.... Right Calf   Left Calf ....

.... Weight   Body Fat ....

Progress Picture: []

This weeks Inspiration:

....

....

....

....

....

. Training Schedule .

Monday:

am ....

pm ....

Tuesday:

am ....

pm ....

Wednesday:

am ....

pm ....

Thursday:

am ....

pm ....

Friday:

am ....

pm ....

Saturday:

am ....

pm ....

Sunday

am ....

pm ....

. APPRECIATION .

.1...

.2...

.3...

W
E
E
K
•
1

M
T
W
T
F
S
S

. FOOD .

Meal 1:

....

....calories: ....

Meal 2:

....

....calories: ....

Meal 3:

....

....calories: ....

Meal 4:

....

....calories: ....

Meal 5:

....

....calories: ....

Meal 6:

....

....calories: ....

....total calories: ....

. W E I G H T • T R A I N I N G .

exercise	set 1	set 2	set 3	set 4	set 5	set 6
......	...... /	...... /	...... /	...... /	...... /	...... / ......
......	...... /	...... /	...... /	...... /	...... /	...... / ......
......	...... /	...... /	...... /	...... /	...... /	...... / ......
......	...... /	...... /	...... /	...... /	...... /	...... / ......
......	...... /	...... /	...... /	...... /	...... /	...... / ......
......	...... /	...... /	...... /	...... /	...... /	...... / ......
......	...... /	...... /	...... /	...... /	...... /	...... / ......
......	...... /	...... /	...... /	...... /	...... /	...... / ......
......	...... /	...... /	...... /	...... /	...... /	...... / ......
......	...... /	...... /	...... /	...... /	...... /	...... / ......

. A E R O B I C .

activity .... duration .... distance .... resistance .... calories

....

....

....

. R E C O V E R Y / S T R E T C H E S .

activity .... duration

....

....

....

....

....

. W A T E R .

. APPRECIATION .

.1..

.2..

.3..

W
E
E
K
.
1

M
T
W
T
F
S
S

. F O O D .

Meal 1:

....

....calories: ....

Meal 2:

....

....calories: ....

Meal 3:

....

....calories: ....

Meal 4:

....

....calories: ....

Meal 5:

....

....calories: ....

Meal 6:

....

....calories: ....

....total calories: ....

. W E I G H T • T R A I N I N G .

exercise	set 1	set 2	set 3	set 4	set 5	set 6
....	...... /	...... /	...... /	...... /	...... /	...... / ......
....	...... /	...... /	...... /	...... /	...... /	...... / ......
....	...... /	...... /	...... /	...... /	...... /	...... / ......
....	...... /	...... /	...... /	...... /	...... /	...... / ......
....	...... /	...... /	...... /	...... /	...... /	...... / ......
....	...... /	...... /	...... /	...... /	...... /	...... / ......
....	...... /	...... /	...... /	...... /	...... /	...... / ......
....	...... /	...... /	...... /	...... /	...... /	...... / ......
....	...... /	...... /	...... /	...... /	...... /	...... / ......
....	...... /	...... /	...... /	...... /	...... /	...... / ......

. A E R O B I C .

activity .... duration .... distance .... resistance .... calories

....
....
....

. R E C O V E R Y / S T R E T C H E S .

activity .... duration

....
....
....
....
....

. W A T E R .

. APPRECIATION .

.1..

.2..

.3..

W
E
E
K
•
1

M
T
W
T
F
S
S

. FOOD .

Meal 1:

....

....calories: ....

Meal 2:

....

....calories: ....

Meal 3:

....

....calories: ....

Meal 4:

....

....calories: ....

Meal 5:

....

....calories: ....

Meal 6:

....

....calories: ....

....total calories: ....

. W E I G H T • T R A I N I N G .

exercise	set 1	set 2	set 3	set 4	set 5	set 6
....	...... /	...... /	...... /	...... /	...... /	...... / ......
....	...... /	...... /	...... /	...... /	...... /	...... / ......
....	...... /	...... /	...... /	...... /	...... /	...... / ......
....	...... /	...... /	...... /	...... /	...... /	...... / ......
....	...... /	...... /	...... /	...... /	...... /	...... / ......
....	...... /	...... /	...... /	...... /	...... /	...... / ......
....	...... /	...... /	...... /	...... /	...... /	...... / ......
....	...... /	...... /	...... /	...... /	...... /	...... / ......
....	...... /	...... /	...... /	...... /	...... /	...... / ......
....	...... /	...... /	...... /	...... /	...... /	...... / ......

. A E R O B I C .

activity .... duration .... distance .... resistance .... calories

....

....

....

. R E C O V E R Y / S T R E T C H E S .

activity .... duration

....

....

....

....

....

. W A T E R .

. APPRECIATION .

.1...

.2...

.3...

W
E
E
K
•
1

M
T
W
T
F
S
S

. F O O D .

Meal 1:
....

....calories: ....

Meal 2:
....

....calories: ....

Meal 3:
....

....calories: ....

Meal 4:
....

....calories: ....

Meal 5:
....

....calories: ....

Meal 6:
....

....calories: ....

....total calories: ....

. W E I G H T • T R A I N I N G .

exercise	set 1	set 2	set 3	set 4	set 5	set 6
......	...... /	...... /	...... /	...... /	...... /	...... / ......
......	...... /	...... /	...... /	...... /	...... /	...... / ......
......	...... /	...... /	...... /	...... /	...... /	...... / ......
......	...... /	...... /	...... /	...... /	...... /	...... / ......
......	...... /	...... /	...... /	...... /	...... /	...... / ......
......	...... /	...... /	...... /	...... /	...... /	...... / ......
......	...... /	...... /	...... /	...... /	...... /	...... / ......
......	...... /	...... /	...... /	...... /	...... /	...... / ......
......	...... /	...... /	...... /	...... /	...... /	...... / ......
......	...... /	...... /	...... /	...... /	...... /	...... / ......

. A E R O B I C .

activity .... duration .... distance .... resistance .... calories

....
....
....

. R E C O V E R Y / S T R E T C H E S .

activity .... duration

....
....
....
....
....

. W A T E R .

. A P P R E C I A T I O N .

.1..

.2..

.3..

W
E
E
K
•
1

M
T
W
T
F
S
S

. F O O D .

Meal 1:

....

....calories: ....

Meal 2:

....

....calories: ....

Meal 3:

....

....calories: ....

Meal 4:

....

....calories: ....

Meal 5:

....

....calories: ....

Meal 6:

....

....calories: ....

....total calories: ....

. W E I G H T • T R A I N I N G.

exercise ...... set 1 ...... set 2 ...... set 3 ...... set 4 ...... set 5 ...... set 6

.... / .... / .... / .... / .... / .... / ......

.... / .... / .... / .... / .... / .... / ......

.... / .... / .... / .... / .... / .... / ......

.... / .... / .... / .... / .... / .... / ......

.... / .... / .... / .... / .... / .... / ......

.... / .... / .... / .... / .... / .... / ......

.... / .... / .... / .... / .... / .... / ......

.... / .... / .... / .... / .... / .... / ......

.... / .... / .... / .... / .... / .... / ......

.... / .... / .... / .... / .... / .... / ......

. A E R O B I C.

activity .... duration .... distance .... resistance .... calories

....

....

....

. R E C O V E R Y / S T R E T C H E S.

activity .... duration

....

....

....

....

....

. W A T E R.

. APPRECIATION .

.1...

.2...

.3...

W
E
E # . F O O D .
K
E ## Meal 1:

....

....calories: ....

Meal 2:

....

....calories: ....

Meal 3:

....

....calories: ....

Meal 4:

....

....calories: ....

Meal 5:

....

....calories: ....

Meal 6:

....

....calories: ....

....total calories: ....

.WEIGHT•TRAINING.

exercise	set 1	set 2	set 3	set 4	set 5	set 6
....	...... /	...... /	...... /	...... /	...... /	...... / ......
....	...... /	...... /	...... /	...... /	...... /	...... / ......
....	...... /	...... /	...... /	...... /	...... /	...... / ......
....	...... /	...... /	...... /	...... /	...... /	...... / ......
....	...... /	...... /	...... /	...... /	...... /	...... / ......
....	...... /	...... /	...... /	...... /	...... /	...... / ......
....	...... /	...... /	...... /	...... /	...... /	...... / ......
....	...... /	...... /	...... /	...... /	...... /	...... / ......
....	...... /	...... /	...... /	...... /	...... /	...... / ......
....	...... /	...... /	...... /	...... /	...... /	...... / ......

.AEROBIC.

activity .... duration .... distance .... resistance .... calories

....
....
....

.RECOVERY/STRETCHES.

activity .... duration

....
....
....
....
....

.WATER.

. A P P R E C I A T I O N .

.1..

.2..

.3..

W
E
E
K

•

1

M
T
W
T
F
S
S

. F O O D .

Meal 1:

....

....calories: ....

Meal 2:

....

....calories: ....

Meal 3:

....

....calories: ....

Meal 4:

....

....calories: ....

Meal 5:

....

....calories: ....

Meal 6:

....

....calories: ....

....total calories: ....

. W E I G H T • T R A I N I N G .

exercise	set 1	set 2	set 3	set 4	set 5	set 6
....	...... /	...... /	...... /	...... /	...... /	...... / ......
....	...... /	...... /	...... /	...... /	...... /	...... / ......
....	...... /	...... /	...... /	...... /	...... /	...... / ......
....	...... /	...... /	...... /	...... /	...... /	...... / ......
....	...... /	...... /	...... /	...... /	...... /	...... / ......
....	...... /	...... /	...... /	...... /	...... /	...... / ......
....	...... /	...... /	...... /	...... /	...... /	...... / ......
....	...... /	...... /	...... /	...... /	...... /	...... / ......
....	...... /	...... /	...... /	...... /	...... /	...... / ......
....	...... /	...... /	...... /	...... /	...... /	...... / ......

. A E R O B I C .

activity .... duration .... distance .... resistance .... calories

....

....

....

. R E C O V E R Y / S T R E T C H E S .

activity .... duration

....

....

....

....

....

. W A T E R .

W E E K · 2

I haven't got time for arguments, bitterness and uncertainties. Life is far too short for things like that.

Goals:

....

....

....

....

....

Measurements:

.... Chest   Waist ....

.... Umbilicus   Hips ....

.... Right Bicep   Left Bicep ....

.... Right Thigh   Left Thigh ....

.... Right Calf   Left Calf ....

.... Weight   Body Fat ....

Progress Picture: []

This weeks Inspiration:

....

....

....

....

....

. Training Schedule .

Monday:

am ....

pm ....

Tuesday:

am ....

pm ....

Wednesday:

am ....

pm ....

Thursday:

am ....

pm ....

Friday:

am ....

pm ....

Saturday:

am ....

pm ....

Sunday

am ....

pm ....

. APPRECIATION .

.1..

.2..

.3..

W
E
E
K
.
1

M
T
W
T
F
S
S

. FOOD .

Meal 1:

....

....calories: ....

Meal 2:

....

....calories: ....

Meal 3:

....

....calories: ....

Meal 4:

....

....calories: ....

Meal 5:

....

....calories: ....

Meal 6:

....

....calories: ....

....total calories: ....

.WEIGHT•TRAINING.

exercise	set 1	set 2	set 3	set 4	set 5	set 6
....	...... /	...... /	...... /	...... /	...... /	...... / ......
....	...... /	...... /	...... /	...... /	...... /	...... / ......
....	...... /	...... /	...... /	...... /	...... /	...... / ......
....	...... /	...... /	...... /	...... /	...... /	...... / ......
....	...... /	...... /	...... /	...... /	...... /	...... / ......
....	...... /	...... /	...... /	...... /	...... /	...... / ......
....	...... /	...... /	...... /	...... /	...... /	...... / ......
....	...... /	...... /	...... /	...... /	...... /	...... / ......
....	...... /	...... /	...... /	...... /	...... /	...... / ......
....	...... /	...... /	...... /	...... /	...... /	...... / ......

.AEROBIC.

activity .... duration .... distance .... resistance .... calories

....

....

....

.RECOVERY/STRETCHES.

activity .... duration

....

....

....

....

....

.WATER.

. APPRECIATION .

.1...

.2...

.3...

W
E
E
K
•
1

M
T
W
T
F
S
S

. F O O D .

Meal 1:

....

....calories: ....

Meal 2:

....

....calories: ....

Meal 3:

....

....calories: ....

Meal 4:

....

....calories: ....

Meal 5:

....

....calories: ....

Meal 6:

....

....calories: ....

....total calories: ....

.WEIGHT•TRAINING.

exercise	set 1	set 2	set 3	set 4	set 5	set 6
......	...... /	...... /	...... /	...... /	...... /	...... / ......
......	...... /	...... /	...... /	...... /	...... /	...... / ......
......	...... /	...... /	...... /	...... /	...... /	...... / ......
......	...... /	...... /	...... /	...... /	...... /	...... / ......
......	...... /	...... /	...... /	...... /	...... /	...... / ......
......	...... /	...... /	...... /	...... /	...... /	...... / ......
......	...... /	...... /	...... /	...... /	...... /	...... / ......
......	...... /	...... /	...... /	...... /	...... /	...... / ......
......	...... /	...... /	...... /	...... /	...... /	...... / ......
......	...... /	...... /	...... /	...... /	...... /	...... / ......

.AEROBIC.

activity .... duration .... distance .... resistance .... calories

....

....

....

.RECOVERY/STRETCHES.

activity .... duration

....

....

....

....

....

.WATER.

. APPRECIATION .

.1..

.2..

.3..

W
E
E
K

.

1

M
T
W
T
F
S
S

. FOOD .

Meal 1:

....

....calories: ....

Meal 2:

....

....calories: ....

Meal 3:

....

....calories: ....

Meal 4:

....

....calories: ....

Meal 5:

....

....calories: ....

Meal 6:

....

....calories: ....

....total calories: ....

.WEIGHT•TRAINING.

exercise	set 1	set 2	set 3	set 4	set 5	set 6
......	...... /	...... /	...... /	...... /	...... /	...... / ......
......	...... /	...... /	...... /	...... /	...... /	...... / ......
......	...... /	...... /	...... /	...... /	...... /	...... / ......
......	...... /	...... /	...... /	...... /	...... /	...... / ......
......	...... /	...... /	...... /	...... /	...... /	...... / ......
......	...... /	...... /	...... /	...... /	...... /	...... / ......
......	...... /	...... /	...... /	...... /	...... /	...... / ......
......	...... /	...... /	...... /	...... /	...... /	...... / ......
......	...... /	...... /	...... /	...... /	...... /	...... / ......
......	...... /	...... /	...... /	...... /	...... /	...... / ......

.AEROBIC.

activity .... duration .... distance .... resistance .... calories

....

....

....

.RECOVERY/STRETCHES.

activity .... duration

....

....

....

....

....

.WATER.

. APPRECIATION .

.1..

.2..

.3..

W
E

. FOOD .

Meal 1:

E

....

K

....calories: ....

Meal 2:

•

....

1

....calories: ....

Meal 3:

M

....

T

....calories: ....

Meal 4:

W

....

T

....calories: ....

F

Meal 5:

S

....

S

....calories: ....

Meal 6:

....

....calories: ....

....total calories: ....

.WEIGHT•TRAINING.

exercise	set 1	set 2	set 3	set 4	set 5	set 6
......	...... /	...... /	...... /	...... /	...... /	...... / ......
......	...... /	...... /	...... /	...... /	...... /	...... / ......
......	...... /	...... /	...... /	...... /	...... /	...... / ......
......	...... /	...... /	...... /	...... /	...... /	...... / ......
......	...... /	...... /	...... /	...... /	...... /	...... / ......
......	...... /	...... /	...... /	...... /	...... /	...... / ......
......	...... /	...... /	...... /	...... /	...... /	...... / ......
......	...... /	...... /	...... /	...... /	...... /	...... / ......
......	...... /	...... /	...... /	...... /	...... /	...... / ......
......	...... /	...... /	...... /	...... /	...... /	...... / ......

.AEROBIC.

activity .... duration .... distance .... resistance .... calories

....

....

....

.RECOVERY/STRETCHES.

activity .... duration

....

....

....

....

....

.WATER.

. APPRECIATION .

.1...

.2...

.3...

W
E
E
K
•
1

M
T
W
T
F
S
S

. FOOD .

Meal 1:

....

....calories: ....

Meal 2:

....

....calories: ....

Meal 3:

....

....calories: ....

Meal 4:

....

....calories: ....

Meal 5:

....

....calories: ....

Meal 6:

....

....calories: ....

....total calories: ....

. W E I G H T • T R A I N I N G .

exercise	set 1	set 2	set 3	set 4	set 5	set 6
....	...... /	...... /	...... /	...... /	...... /	...... / ......
....	...... /	...... /	...... /	...... /	...... /	...... / ......
....	...... /	...... /	...... /	...... /	...... /	...... / ......
....	...... /	...... /	...... /	...... /	...... /	...... / ......
....	...... /	...... /	...... /	...... /	...... /	...... / ......
....	...... /	...... /	...... /	...... /	...... /	...... / ......
....	...... /	...... /	...... /	...... /	...... /	...... / ......
....	...... /	...... /	...... /	...... /	...... /	...... / ......
....	...... /	...... /	...... /	...... /	...... /	...... / ......
....	...... /	...... /	...... /	...... /	...... /	...... / ......

. A E R O B I C .

activity .... duration .... distance .... resistance .... calories

....

....

....

. R E C O V E R Y / S T R E T C H E S .

activity .... duration

....

....

....

....

....

. W A T E R .

. APPRECIATION .

.1..

.2..

.3..

W
E
E
K
•
1

M
T
W
T
F
S
S

. F O O D .

Meal 1:

....

....calories: ....

Meal 2:

....

....calories: ....

Meal 3:

....

....calories: ....

Meal 4:

....

....calories: ....

Meal 5:

....

....calories: ....

Meal 6:

....

....calories: ....

....total calories: ....

.WEIGHT•TRAINING.

exercise	set 1	set 2	set 3	set 4	set 5	set 6
....	...... /	...... /	...... /	...... /	...... /	...... / ......
....	...... /	...... /	...... /	...... /	...... /	...... / ......
....	...... /	...... /	...... /	...... /	...... /	...... / ......
....	...... /	...... /	...... /	...... /	...... /	...... / ......
....	...... /	...... /	...... /	...... /	...... /	...... / ......
....	...... /	...... /	...... /	...... /	...... /	...... / ......
....	...... /	...... /	...... /	...... /	...... /	...... / ......
....	...... /	...... /	...... /	...... /	...... /	...... / ......
....	...... /	...... /	...... /	...... /	...... /	...... / ......
....	...... /	...... /	...... /	...... /	...... /	...... / ......

.AEROBIC.

activity .... duration .... distance .... resistance .... calories

....

....

....

.RECOVERY/STRETCHES.

activity .... duration

....

....

....

....

....

.WATER.

. APPRECIATION .

.1..

.2..

.3..

W
E
E
K
.
1

M
T
W
T
F
S
S

. FOOD .

Meal 1:

....

....calories: ....

Meal 2:

....

....calories: ....

Meal 3:

....

....calories: ....

Meal 4:

....

....calories: ....

Meal 5:

....

....calories: ....

Meal 6:

....

....calories: ....

....total calories: ....

. W E I G H T • T R A I N I N G .

exercise	set 1	set 2	set 3	set 4	set 5	set 6
....	...... /	...... /	...... /	...... /	...... /	...... / ......
....	...... /	...... /	...... /	...... /	...... /	...... / ......
....	...... /	...... /	...... /	...... /	...... /	...... / ......
....	...... /	...... /	...... /	...... /	...... /	...... / ......
....	...... /	...... /	...... /	...... /	...... /	...... / ......
....	...... /	...... /	...... /	...... /	...... /	...... / ......
....	...... /	...... /	...... /	...... /	...... /	...... / ......
....	...... /	...... /	...... /	...... /	...... /	...... / ......
....	...... /	...... /	...... /	...... /	...... /	...... / ......
....	...... /	...... /	...... /	...... /	...... /	...... / ......

. A E R O B I C .

activity .... duration .... distance .... resistance .... calories

....

....

....

. R E C O V E R Y / S T R E T C H E S .

activity .... duration

....

....

....

....

....

. W A T E R .

WEEK

• 3

I have not failed. I've just found 10,000 ways that won't work.

Goals:

....

....

....

....

....

Measurements:

.... Chest   Waist ....

.... Umbilicus   Hips ....

.... Right Bicep   Left Bicep ....

.... Right Thigh   Left Thigh ....

.... Right Calf   Left Calf ....

.... Weight   Body Fat ....

Progress Picture: []

This weeks Inspiration:

....

....

....

....

....

. Training Schedule .

Monday:

am ....

pm ....

Tuesday:

am ....

pm ....

Wednesday:

am ....

pm ....

Thursday:

am ....

pm ....

Friday:

am ....

pm ....

Saturday:

am ....

pm ....

Sunday

am ....

pm ....

. A P P R E C I A T I O N .

.1...

.2...

.3...

W
E
E
K
•
1

M
T
W
T
F
S
S

. F O O D .

Meal 1:

....

....calories: ....

Meal 2:

....

....calories: ....

Meal 3:

....

....calories: ....

Meal 4:

....

....calories: ....

Meal 5:

....

....calories: ....

Meal 6:

....

....calories: ....

....total calories: ....

.WEIGHT•TRAINING.

exercise	set 1	set 2	set 3	set 4	set 5	set 6
....	...... /	...... /	...... /	...... /	...... /	...... / ......
....	...... /	...... /	...... /	...... /	...... /	...... / ......
....	...... /	...... /	...... /	...... /	...... /	...... / ......
....	...... /	...... /	...... /	...... /	...... /	...... / ......
....	...... /	...... /	...... /	...... /	...... /	...... / ......
....	...... /	...... /	...... /	...... /	...... /	...... / ......
....	...... /	...... /	...... /	...... /	...... /	...... / ......
....	...... /	...... /	...... /	...... /	...... /	...... / ......
....	...... /	...... /	...... /	...... /	...... /	...... / ......
....	...... /	...... /	...... /	...... /	...... /	...... / ......

.AEROBIC.

activity .... duration .... distance .... resistance .... calories

....

....

....

.RECOVERY/STRETCHES.

activity .... duration

....

....

....

....

....

.WATER.

. APPRECIATION .

.1..

.2..

.3..

W
E
E
K
•
1

M
T
W
T
F
S
S

. F O O D .

Meal 1:

....

....calories: ....

Meal 2:

....

....calories: ....

Meal 3:

....

....calories: ....

Meal 4:

....

....calories: ....

Meal 5:

....

....calories: ....

Meal 6:

....

....calories: ....

....total calories: ....

. W E I G H T • T R A I N I N G .

exercise	set 1	set 2	set 3	set 4	set 5	set 6
....	...... /	...... /	...... /	...... /	...... /	...... / ......
....	...... /	...... /	...... /	...... /	...... /	...... / ......
....	...... /	...... /	...... /	...... /	...... /	...... / ......
....	...... /	...... /	...... /	...... /	...... /	...... / ......
....	...... /	...... /	...... /	...... /	...... /	...... / ......
....	...... /	...... /	...... /	...... /	...... /	...... / ......
....	...... /	...... /	...... /	...... /	...... /	...... / ......
....	...... /	...... /	...... /	...... /	...... /	...... / ......
....	...... /	...... /	...... /	...... /	...... /	...... / ......
....	...... /	...... /	...... /	...... /	...... /	...... / ......

. A E R O B I C .

activity .... duration .... distance .... resistance .... calories

....

....

....

. R E C O V E R Y / S T R E T C H E S .

activity .... duration

....

....

....

....

....

. W A T E R .

. APPRECIATION .

.1..

.2..

.3..

W
E
                . F O O D .
E
            Meal 1:

....

....calories: ....

            Meal 2:

K

•

1
....

....calories: ....

            Meal 3:

M
....

T
....calories: ....

            Meal 4:

W

T
....

....calories: ....

F
            Meal 5:

S
....

S
....calories: ....

            Meal 6:

....

....calories: ....

....total calories: ....

.WEIGHT•TRAINING.

exercise	set 1	set 2	set 3	set 4	set 5	set 6
....	...... /	...... /	...... /	...... /	...... /	...... / ......
....	...... /	...... /	...... /	...... /	...... /	...... / ......
....	...... /	...... /	...... /	...... /	...... /	...... / ......
....	...... /	...... /	...... /	...... /	...... /	...... / ......
....	...... /	...... /	...... /	...... /	...... /	...... / ......
....	...... /	...... /	...... /	...... /	...... /	...... / ......
....	...... /	...... /	...... /	...... /	...... /	...... / ......
....	...... /	...... /	...... /	...... /	...... /	...... / ......
....	...... /	...... /	...... /	...... /	...... /	...... / ......
....	...... /	...... /	...... /	...... /	...... /	...... / ......

.AEROBIC.

activity .... **duration** .... **distance** .... **resistance** .... **calories**

....

....

....

.RECOVERY/STRETCHES.

activity .... **duration**

....

....

....

....

....

.WATER.

. APPRECIATION .

.1...

.2...

.3...

W
E
E
K
.
1

M
T
W
T
F
S
S

. FOOD .

Meal 1:

....

....calories: ....

Meal 2:

....

....calories: ....

Meal 3:

....

....calories: ....

Meal 4:

....

....calories: ....

Meal 5:

....

....calories: ....

Meal 6:

....

....calories: ....

....total calories: ....

. W E I G H T • T R A I N I N G .

exercise	set 1	set 2	set 3	set 4	set 5	set 6
....	...... /	...... /	...... /	...... /	...... /	...... / ......
....	...... /	...... /	...... /	...... /	...... /	...... / ......
....	...... /	...... /	...... /	...... /	...... /	...... / ......
....	...... /	...... /	...... /	...... /	...... /	...... / ......
....	...... /	...... /	...... /	...... /	...... /	...... / ......
....	...... /	...... /	...... /	...... /	...... /	...... / ......
....	...... /	...... /	...... /	...... /	...... /	...... / ......
....	...... /	...... /	...... /	...... /	...... /	...... / ......
....	...... /	...... /	...... /	...... /	...... /	...... / ......
....	...... /	...... /	...... /	...... /	...... /	...... / ......

. A E R O B I C .

activity .... duration .... distance .... resistance .... calories

....

....

....

. R E C O V E R Y / S T R E T C H E S .

activity .... duration

....

....

....

....

....

. W A T E R .

. APPRECIATION .

.1..

.2..

.3..

W
E
E
K

•

1

M
T
W
T
F
S
S

. FOOD .

Meal 1:

....

....calories: ....

Meal 2:

....

....calories: ....

Meal 3:

....

....calories: ....

Meal 4:

....

....calories: ....

Meal 5:

....

....calories: ....

Meal 6:

....

....calories: ....

....total calories: ....

.WEIGHT•TRAINING.

exercise	set 1	set 2	set 3	set 4	set 5	set 6
....	...... /	...... /	...... /	...... /	...... /	...... / ......
....	...... /	...... /	...... /	...... /	...... /	...... / ......
....	...... /	...... /	...... /	...... /	...... /	...... / ......
....	...... /	...... /	...... /	...... /	...... /	...... / ......
....	...... /	...... /	...... /	...... /	...... /	...... / ......
....	...... /	...... /	...... /	...... /	...... /	...... / ......
....	...... /	...... /	...... /	...... /	...... /	...... / ......
....	...... /	...... /	...... /	...... /	...... /	...... / ......
....	...... /	...... /	...... /	...... /	...... /	...... / ......
....	...... /	...... /	...... /	...... /	...... /	...... / ......

.AEROBIC.

activity .... duration .... distance .... resistance .... calories

....

....

....

.RECOVERY/STRETCHES.

activity .... duration

....

....

....

....

....

.WATER.

. APPRECIATION.

.1...

.2...

.3...

W
E
E
K
•
1

M
T
W
T
F
S
S

.FOOD.

Meal 1:

....

....calories: ....

Meal 2:

....

....calories: ....

Meal 3:

....

....calories: ....

Meal 4:

....

....calories: ....

Meal 5:

....

....calories: ....

Meal 6:

....

....calories: ....

....total calories: ....

.WEIGHT•TRAINING.

exercise	set 1	set 2	set 3	set 4	set 5	set 6
....	...... /	...... /	...... /	...... /	...... /	...... / ......
....	...... /	...... /	...... /	...... /	...... /	...... / ......
....	...... /	...... /	...... /	...... /	...... /	...... / ......
....	...... /	...... /	...... /	...... /	...... /	...... / ......
....	...... /	...... /	...... /	...... /	...... /	...... / ......
....	...... /	...... /	...... /	...... /	...... /	...... / ......
....	...... /	...... /	...... /	...... /	...... /	...... / ......
....	...... /	...... /	...... /	...... /	...... /	...... / ......
....	...... /	...... /	...... /	...... /	...... /	...... / ......
....	...... /	...... /	...... /	...... /	...... /	...... / ......

.AEROBIC.

activity .... duration .... distance .... resistance .... calories

....

....

....

.RECOVERY/STRETCHES.

activity .... duration

....

....

....

....

....

.WATER.

. APPRECIATION .

.1...

.2...

.3...

W
E
E
K
•
1

M
T
W
T
F
S
S

.FOOD.

Meal 1:

....

....calories: ....

Meal 2:

....

....calories: ....

Meal 3:

....

....calories: ....

Meal 4:

....

....calories: ....

Meal 5:

....

....calories: ....

Meal 6:

....

....calories: ....

....total calories: ....

. W E I G H T • T R A I N I N G .

exercise ...... set 1 ...... set 2 ...... set 3 ...... set 4 ...... set 5 ...... set 6

.... / .... / .... / .... / .... / .... / ......

.... / .... / .... / .... / .... / .... / ......

.... / .... / .... / .... / .... / .... / ......

.... / .... / .... / .... / .... / .... / ......

.... / .... / .... / .... / .... / .... / ......

.... / .... / .... / .... / .... / .... / ......

.... / .... / .... / .... / .... / .... / ......

.... / .... / .... / .... / .... / .... / ......

.... / .... / .... / .... / .... / .... / ......

.... / .... / .... / .... / .... / .... / ......

. A E R O B I C .

activity .... duration .... distance .... resistance .... calories

....

....

....

. R E C O V E R Y / S T R E T C H E S .

activity .... duration

....

....

....

....

....

. W A T E R .

WEEK · 4

Never let small minds convince you that your dreams are too big.

Goals:

....

....

....

....

....

Measurements:

.... Chest   Waist ....

.... Umbilicus   Hips ....

.... Right Bicep   Left Bicep ....

.... Right Thigh   Left Thigh ....

.... Right Calf   Left Calf ....

.... Weight   Body Fat ....

Progress Picture: []

This weeks Inspiration:

....

....

....

....

....

. Training Schedule .

Monday:

am ....

pm ....

Tuesday:

am ....

pm ....

Wednesday:

am ....

pm ....

Thursday:

am ....

pm ....

Friday:

am ....

pm ....

Saturday:

am ....

pm ....

Sunday

am ....

pm ....

. APPRECIATION .

.1...

.2...

.3...

W
E

.FOOD.

Meal 1:

E
....

K
....calories: ....

●

Meal 2:

1
....

....calories: ....

Meal 3:

M
....

T
....calories: ....

Meal 4:

W

T
....

....calories: ....

F

Meal 5:

S
....

S
....calories: ....

Meal 6:

....

....calories: ....

....total calories: ....

.WEIGHT•TRAINING.

exercise	set 1	set 2	set 3	set 4	set 5	set 6
......	..... /	..... /	..... /	..... /	..... /	..... / .....
......	..... /	..... /	..... /	..... /	..... /	..... / .....
......	..... /	..... /	..... /	..... /	..... /	..... / .....
......	..... /	..... /	..... /	..... /	..... /	..... / .....
......	..... /	..... /	..... /	..... /	..... /	..... / .....
......	..... /	..... /	..... /	..... /	..... /	..... / .....
......	..... /	..... /	..... /	..... /	..... /	..... / .....
......	..... /	..... /	..... /	..... /	..... /	..... / .....
......	..... /	..... /	..... /	..... /	..... /	..... / .....
......	..... /	..... /	..... /	..... /	..... /	..... / .....

.AEROBIC.

activity .... duration .... distance .... resistance .... calories

....

....

....

.RECOVERY/STRETCHES.

activity .... duration

....

....

....

....

....

.WATER.

. APPRECIATION .

.1...

.2...

.3...

W
E
E
K
.
1

M
T
W
T
F
S
S

. FOOD .

Meal 1:

....

....calories: ....

Meal 2:

....

....calories: ....

Meal 3:

....

....calories: ....

Meal 4:

....

....calories: ....

Meal 5:

....

....calories: ....

Meal 6:

....

....calories: ....

....total calories: ....

.WEIGHT•TRAINING.

exercise	set 1	set 2	set 3	set 4	set 5	set 6
....	...... /	...... /	...... /	...... /	...... /	...... / ......
....	...... /	...... /	...... /	...... /	...... /	...... / ......
....	...... /	...... /	...... /	...... /	...... /	...... / ......
....	...... /	...... /	...... /	...... /	...... /	...... / ......
....	...... /	...... /	...... /	...... /	...... /	...... / ......
....	...... /	...... /	...... /	...... /	...... /	...... / ......
....	...... /	...... /	...... /	...... /	...... /	...... / ......
....	...... /	...... /	...... /	...... /	...... /	...... / ......
....	...... /	...... /	...... /	...... /	...... /	...... / ......
....	...... /	...... /	...... /	...... /	...... /	...... / ......

.AEROBIC.

activity .... duration .... distance .... resistance .... calories

....

....

....

.RECOVERY/STRETCHES.

activity .... duration

....

....

....

....

....

.WATER.

. APPRECIATION.

.1..

.2..

.3..

W
E
E
K
.
1

M
T
W
T
F
S
S

.FOOD.

Meal 1:

....

....calories: ....

Meal 2:

....

....calories: ....

Meal 3:

....

....calories: ....

Meal 4:

....

....calories: ....

Meal 5:

....

....calories: ....

Meal 6:

....

....calories: ....

....total calories: ....

. W E I G H T • T R A I N I N G .

exercise	set 1	set 2	set 3	set 4	set 5	set 6
......	...... /	...... /	...... /	...... /	...... /	...... / ......
......	...... /	...... /	...... /	...... /	...... /	...... / ......
......	...... /	...... /	...... /	...... /	...... /	...... / ......
......	...... /	...... /	...... /	...... /	...... /	...... / ......
......	...... /	...... /	...... /	...... /	...... /	...... / ......
......	...... /	...... /	...... /	...... /	...... /	...... / ......
......	...... /	...... /	...... /	...... /	...... /	...... / ......
......	...... /	...... /	...... /	...... /	...... /	...... / ......
......	...... /	...... /	...... /	...... /	...... /	...... / ......
......	...... /	...... /	...... /	...... /	...... /	...... / ......

. A E R O B I C .

activity .... duration .... distance .... resistance .... calories

....

....

....

. R E C O V E R Y / S T R E T C H E S .

activity .... duration

....

....

....

....

....

. W A T E R .

. APPRECIATION .

.1..

.2..

.3..

W
E
E
K
•
1

M
T
W
T
F
S
S

. F O O D .

Meal 1:

....

....calories: ....

Meal 2:

....

....calories: ....

Meal 3:

....

....calories: ....

Meal 4:

....

....calories: ....

Meal 5:

....

....calories: ....

Meal 6:

....

....calories: ....

....total calories: ....

.WEIGHT•TRAINING.

exercise	set 1	set 2	set 3	set 4	set 5	set 6
....	...... /	...... /	...... /	...... /	...... /	...... / ......
....	...... /	...... /	...... /	...... /	...... /	...... / ......
....	...... /	...... /	...... /	...... /	...... /	...... / ......
....	...... /	...... /	...... /	...... /	...... /	...... / ......
....	...... /	...... /	...... /	...... /	...... /	...... / ......
....	...... /	...... /	...... /	...... /	...... /	...... / ......
....	...... /	...... /	...... /	...... /	...... /	...... / ......
....	...... /	...... /	...... /	...... /	...... /	...... / ......
....	...... /	...... /	...... /	...... /	...... /	...... / ......
....	...... /	...... /	...... /	...... /	...... /	...... / ......

.AEROBIC.

activity .... duration .... distance .... resistance .... calories

....

....

....

.RECOVERY/STRETCHES.

activity .... duration

....

....

....

....

....

.WATER.

. APPRECIATION .

.1..

.2..

.3..

W
E
E
K
●
1

M
T
W
T
F
S
S

. FOOD .

Meal 1:

....

....calories: ....

Meal 2:

....

....calories: ....

Meal 3:

....

....calories: ....

Meal 4:

....

....calories: ....

Meal 5:

....

....calories: ....

Meal 6:

....

....calories: ....

....total calories: ....

. W E I G H T • T R A I N I N G .

exercise	set 1	set 2	set 3	set 4	set 5	set 6
....	...... /	...... /	...... /	...... /	...... /	...... / ......
....	...... /	...... /	...... /	...... /	...... /	...... / ......
....	...... /	...... /	...... /	...... /	...... /	...... / ......
....	...... /	...... /	...... /	...... /	...... /	...... / ......
....	...... /	...... /	...... /	...... /	...... /	...... / ......
....	...... /	...... /	...... /	...... /	...... /	...... / ......
....	...... /	...... /	...... /	...... /	...... /	...... / ......
....	...... /	...... /	...... /	...... /	...... /	...... / ......
....	...... /	...... /	...... /	...... /	...... /	...... / ......
....	...... /	...... /	...... /	...... /	...... /	...... / ......

. A E R O B I C .

activity .... duration .... distance .... resistance .... calories

....

....

....

. R E C O V E R Y / S T R E T C H E S .

activity .... duration

....

....

....

....

....

. W A T E R .

. APPRECIATION .

.1..

.2..

.3..

W
E
E
K

•

1

M
T
W
T
F
S
S

. FOOD .

Meal 1:

....

....calories: ....

Meal 2:

....

....calories: ....

Meal 3:

....

....calories: ....

Meal 4:

....

....calories: ....

Meal 5:

....

....calories: ....

Meal 6:

....

....calories: ....

....total calories: ....

. W E I G H T • T R A I N I N G .

exercise	set 1	set 2	set 3	set 4	set 5	set 6
....	...... /	...... /	...... /	...... /	...... /	...... / ......
....	...... /	...... /	...... /	...... /	...... /	...... / ......
....	...... /	...... /	...... /	...... /	...... /	...... / ......
....	...... /	...... /	...... /	...... /	...... /	...... / ......
....	...... /	...... /	...... /	...... /	...... /	...... / ......
....	...... /	...... /	...... /	...... /	...... /	...... / ......
....	...... /	...... /	...... /	...... /	...... /	...... / ......
....	...... /	...... /	...... /	...... /	...... /	...... / ......
....	...... /	...... /	...... /	...... /	...... /	...... / ......
....	...... /	...... /	...... /	...... /	...... /	...... / ......

. A E R O B I C .

activity .... duration .... distance .... resistance .... calories

....

....

....

. R E C O V E R Y / S T R E T C H E S .

activity .... duration

....

....

....

....

....

. W A T E R .

. APPRECIATION .

.1...

.2...

.3...

W
E
E
K
•
1

M
T
W
T
F
S
S

.FOOD.

Meal 1:

....

....calories: ....

Meal 2:

....

....calories: ....

Meal 3:

....

....calories: ....

Meal 4:

....

....calories: ....

Meal 5:

....

....calories: ....

Meal 6:

....

....calories: ....

....total calories: ....

. W E I G H T • T R A I N I N G .

exercise	set 1	set 2	set 3	set 4	set 5	set 6
....	...... /	...... /	...... /	...... /	...... /	...... / ......
....	...... /	...... /	...... /	...... /	...... /	...... / ......
....	...... /	...... /	...... /	...... /	...... /	...... / ......
....	...... /	...... /	...... /	...... /	...... /	...... / ......
....	...... /	...... /	...... /	...... /	...... /	...... / ......
....	...... /	...... /	...... /	...... /	...... /	...... / ......
....	...... /	...... /	...... /	...... /	...... /	...... / ......
....	...... /	...... /	...... /	...... /	...... /	...... / ......
....	...... /	...... /	...... /	...... /	...... /	...... / ......
....	...... /	...... /	...... /	...... /	...... /	...... / ......

. A E R O B I C .

activity .... duration .... distance .... resistance .... calories

....

....

....

. R E C O V E R Y / S T R E T C H E S .

activity .... duration

....

....

....

....

....

. W A T E R .

W E E K . 5

Learn from yesterday, live for today, hope for tomorrow. The important thing is not to stop questioning.

Goals:

....

....

....

....

....

Measurements:

.... Chest   Waist ....

.... Umbilicus   Hips ....

.... Right Bicep   Left Bicep ....

.... Right Thigh   Left Thigh ....

.... Right Calf   Left Calf ....

.... Weight   Body Fat ....

Progress Picture: []

This weeks Inspiration:

....

....

....

....

....

. Training Schedule .

Monday:

am ....

pm ....

Tuesday:

am ....

pm ....

Wednesday:

am ....

pm ....

Thursday:

am ....

pm ....

Friday:

am ....

pm ....

Saturday:

am ....

pm ....

Sunday

am ....

pm ....

. APPRECIATION .

.1..

.2..

.3..

W
E
E
K
•
1

M
T
W
T
F
S
S

.FOOD.

Meal 1:

....

....calories: ....

Meal 2:

....

....calories: ....

Meal 3:

....

....calories: ....

Meal 4:

....

....calories: ....

Meal 5:

....

....calories: ....

Meal 6:

....

....calories: ....

....total calories: ....

.WEIGHT•TRAINING.

exercise	set 1	set 2	set 3	set 4	set 5	set 6
....	...... /	...... /	...... /	...... /	...... /	...... / ......
....	...... /	...... /	...... /	...... /	...... /	...... / ......
....	...... /	...... /	...... /	...... /	...... /	...... / ......
....	...... /	...... /	...... /	...... /	...... /	...... / ......
....	...... /	...... /	...... /	...... /	...... /	...... / ......
....	...... /	...... /	...... /	...... /	...... /	...... / ......
....	...... /	...... /	...... /	...... /	...... /	...... / ......
....	...... /	...... /	...... /	...... /	...... /	...... / ......
....	...... /	...... /	...... /	...... /	...... /	...... / ......
....	...... /	...... /	...... /	...... /	...... /	...... / ......

.AEROBIC.

activity .... duration .... distance .... resistance .... calories

....

....

....

.RECOVERY/STRETCHES.

activity .... duration

....

....

....

....

....

.WATER.

. APPRECIATION .

.1..

.2..

.3..

W
E
E
K

•

1

M
T
W
T
F
S
S

. F O O D .

Meal 1:

....

....calories: ....

Meal 2:

....

....calories: ....

Meal 3:

....

....calories: ....

Meal 4:

....

....calories: ....

Meal 5:

....

....calories: ....

Meal 6:

....

....calories: ....

....total calories: ....

.WEIGHT•TRAINING.

exercise ...... set 1 ...... set 2 ...... set 3 ...... set 4 ...... set 5 ...... set 6

.... / .... / .... / .... / .... / .... / ......

.... / .... / .... / .... / .... / .... / ......

.... / .... / .... / .... / .... / .... / ......

.... / .... / .... / .... / .... / .... / ......

.... / .... / .... / .... / .... / .... / ......

.... / .... / .... / .... / .... / .... / ......

.... / .... / .... / .... / .... / .... / ......

.... / .... / .... / .... / .... / .... / ......

.... / .... / .... / .... / .... / .... / ......

.... / .... / .... / .... / .... / .... / ......

.AEROBIC.

activity .... duration .... distance .... resistance .... calories

....

....

....

.RECOVERY/STRETCHES.

activity .... duration

....

....

....

....

....

.WATER.

. APPRECIATION .

.1...

.2...

.3...

W
E
E
K
•
1

M
T
W
T
F
S
S

.FOOD.

Meal 1:

....

....calories: ....

Meal 2:

....

....calories: ....

Meal 3:

....

....calories: ....

Meal 4:

....

....calories: ....

Meal 5:

....

....calories: ....

Meal 6:

....

....calories: ....

....total calories: ....

.WEIGHT•TRAINING.

exercise	set 1	set 2	set 3	set 4	set 5	set 6
....	...... /	...... /	...... /	...... /	...... /	...... / ......
....	...... /	...... /	...... /	...... /	...... /	...... / ......
....	...... /	...... /	...... /	...... /	...... /	...... / ......
....	...... /	...... /	...... /	...... /	...... /	...... / ......
....	...... /	...... /	...... /	...... /	...... /	...... / ......
....	...... /	...... /	...... /	...... /	...... /	...... / ......
....	...... /	...... /	...... /	...... /	...... /	...... / ......
....	...... /	...... /	...... /	...... /	...... /	...... / ......
....	...... /	...... /	...... /	...... /	...... /	...... / ......
....	...... /	...... /	...... /	...... /	...... /	...... / ......

.AEROBIC.

activity .... duration .... distance .... resistance .... calories

....

....

....

.RECOVERY/STRETCHES.

activity .... duration

....

....

....

....

....

.WATER.

. APPRECIATION .

.1..

.2..

.3..

W
E
E
K
•
1

M
T
W
T
F
S
S

.FOOD.

Meal 1:

....

....calories: ....

Meal 2:

....

....calories: ....

Meal 3:

....

....calories: ....

Meal 4:

....

....calories: ....

Meal 5:

....

....calories: ....

Meal 6:

....

....calories: ....

....total calories: ....

. W E I G H T • T R A I N I N G .

exercise ...... set 1 ...... set 2 ...... set 3 ...... set 4 ...... set 5 ...... set 6

.... / .... / .... / .... / .... / .... / ......

.... / .... / .... / .... / .... / .... / ......

.... / .... / .... / .... / .... / .... / ......

.... / .... / .... / .... / .... / .... / ......

.... / .... / .... / .... / .... / .... / ......

.... / .... / .... / .... / .... / .... / ......

.... / .... / .... / .... / .... / .... / ......

.... / .... / .... / .... / .... / .... / ......

.... / .... / .... / .... / .... / .... / ......

.... / .... / .... / .... / .... / .... / ......

. A E R O B I C .

activity .... duration .... distance .... resistance .... calories

....

....

....

. R E C O V E R Y / S T R E T C H E S .

activity .... duration

....

....

....

....

....

. W A T E R .

. APPRECIATION .

.1...

.2...

.3...

W
E

.FOOD.

E

Meal 1:

K
....

....calories: ....

•

Meal 2:

1
....

....calories: ....

Meal 3:

M
....

T
....calories: ....

Meal 4:

W
....

T
....calories: ....

F

Meal 5:

S
....

S
....calories: ....

Meal 6:

....

....calories: ....

....total calories: ....

. W E I G H T • T R A I N I N G .

exercise ...... set 1 ...... set 2 ...... set 3 ...... set 4 ...... set 5 ...... set 6

.... / .... / .... / .... / .... / .... / ......

.... / .... / .... / .... / .... / .... / ......

.... / .... / .... / .... / .... / .... / ......

.... / .... / .... / .... / .... / .... / ......

.... / .... / .... / .... / .... / .... / ......

.... / .... / .... / .... / .... / .... / ......

.... / .... / .... / .... / .... / .... / ......

.... / .... / .... / .... / .... / .... / ......

.... / .... / .... / .... / .... / .... / ......

.... / .... / .... / .... / .... / .... / ......

. A E R O B I C .

activity .... duration .... distance .... resistance .... calories

....

....

....

. R E C O V E R Y / S T R E T C H E S .

activity .... duration

....

....

....

....

....

. W A T E R .

. APPRECIATION .

.1..

.2..

.3..

W
E
E
K

•

1

M
T
W
T
F
S
S

. FOOD .

Meal 1:

....

....calories: ....

Meal 2:

....

....calories: ....

Meal 3:

....

....calories: ....

Meal 4:

....

....calories: ....

Meal 5:

....

....calories: ....

Meal 6:

....

....

....calories: ....

....total calories: ....

. W E I G H T • T R A I N I N G .

exercise	set 1	set 2	set 3	set 4	set 5	set 6
....	...... /	...... /	...... /	...... /	...... /	...... / ......
....	...... /	...... /	...... /	...... /	...... /	...... / ......
....	...... /	...... /	...... /	...... /	...... /	...... / ......
....	...... /	...... /	...... /	...... /	...... /	...... / ......
....	...... /	...... /	...... /	...... /	...... /	...... / ......
....	...... /	...... /	...... /	...... /	...... /	...... / ......
....	...... /	...... /	...... /	...... /	...... /	...... / ......
....	...... /	...... /	...... /	...... /	...... /	...... / ......
....	...... /	...... /	...... /	...... /	...... /	...... / ......
....	...... /	...... /	...... /	...... /	...... /	...... / ......

. A E R O B I C .

activity .... duration .... distance .... resistance .... calories

....

....

....

. R E C O V E R Y / S T R E T C H E S .

activity .... duration

....

....

....

....

....

. W A T E R .

. A P P R E C I A T I O N .

.1..

.2..

.3..

W
E
E
K
•
1

M
T
W
T
F
S
S

. F O O D .

Meal 1:
....

....calories: ....

Meal 2:
....

....calories: ....

Meal 3:
....

....calories: ....

Meal 4:
....

....calories: ....

Meal 5:
....

....calories: ....

Meal 6:
....

....calories: ....

....total calories: ....

. W E I G H T • T R A I N I N G .

exercise	set 1	set 2	set 3	set 4	set 5	set 6
....	...... /	...... /	...... /	...... /	...... /	...... / ......
....	...... /	...... /	...... /	...... /	...... /	...... / ......
....	...... /	...... /	...... /	...... /	...... /	...... / ......
....	...... /	...... /	...... /	...... /	...... /	...... / ......
....	...... /	...... /	...... /	...... /	...... /	...... / ......
....	...... /	...... /	...... /	...... /	...... /	...... / ......
....	...... /	...... /	...... /	...... /	...... /	...... / ......
....	...... /	...... /	...... /	...... /	...... /	...... / ......
....	...... /	...... /	...... /	...... /	...... /	...... / ......
....	...... /	...... /	...... /	...... /	...... /	...... / ......

. A E R O B I C .

activity .... duration .... distance .... resistance .... calories

....

....

....

. R E C O V E R Y / S T R E T C H E S .

activity .... duration

....

....

....

....

....

. W A T E R .

WEEK . 6

Either you run the day or the day runs you.

Goals:

....

....

....

....

....

Measurements:

.... Chest   Waist ....

.... Umbilicus   Hips ....

.... Right Bicep   Left Bicep ....

.... Right Thigh   Left Thigh ....

.... Right Calf   Left Calf ....

.... Weight   Body Fat ....

Progress Picture: []

This weeks Inspiration:

....

....

....

....

....

. Training Schedule .

Monday:

am ....

pm ....

Tuesday:

am ....

pm ....

Wednesday:

am ....

pm ....

Thursday:

am ....

pm ....

Friday:

am ....

pm ....

Saturday:

am ....

pm ....

Sunday

am ....

pm ....

. APPRECIATION .

.1..

.2..

.3..

W
E
E
K
•
1

M
T
W
T
F
S
S

. FOOD .

Meal 1:

....

....calories: ....

Meal 2:

....

....calories: ....

Meal 3:

....

....calories: ....

Meal 4:

....

....calories: ....

Meal 5:

....

....calories: ....

Meal 6:

....

....calories: ....

....total calories: ....

.WEIGHT•TRAINING.

exercise	set 1	set 2	set 3	set 4	set 5	set 6
....	.... /	.... /	.... /	.... /	.... /	.... / ......
....	.... /	.... /	.... /	.... /	.... /	.... / ......
....	.... /	.... /	.... /	.... /	.... /	.... / ......
....	.... /	.... /	.... /	.... /	.... /	.... / ......
....	.... /	.... /	.... /	.... /	.... /	.... / ......
....	.... /	.... /	.... /	.... /	.... /	.... / ......
....	.... /	.... /	.... /	.... /	.... /	.... / ......
....	.... /	.... /	.... /	.... /	.... /	.... / ......
....	.... /	.... /	.... /	.... /	.... /	.... / ......
....	.... /	.... /	.... /	.... /	.... /	.... / ......

.AEROBIC.

activity .... duration .... distance .... resistance .... calories

....

....

....

.RECOVERY/STRETCHES.

activity .... duration

....

....

....

....

....

.WATER.

. APPRECIATION .

.1...

.2...

.3...

W
E
E
K
•
1

M
T
W
T
F
S
S

.FOOD.

Meal 1:

....

....calories: ....

Meal 2:

....

....calories: ....

Meal 3:

....

....calories: ....

Meal 4:

....

....calories: ....

Meal 5:

....

....calories: ....

Meal 6:

....

....calories: ....

....total calories: ....

.WEIGHT•TRAINING.

exercise	set 1	set 2	set 3	set 4	set 5	set 6
....	...... /	...... /	...... /	...... /	...... /	...... / ......
....	...... /	...... /	...... /	...... /	...... /	...... / ......
....	...... /	...... /	...... /	...... /	...... /	...... / ......
....	...... /	...... /	...... /	...... /	...... /	...... / ......
....	...... /	...... /	...... /	...... /	...... /	...... / ......
....	...... /	...... /	...... /	...... /	...... /	...... / ......
....	...... /	...... /	...... /	...... /	...... /	...... / ......
....	...... /	...... /	...... /	...... /	...... /	...... / ......
....	...... /	...... /	...... /	...... /	...... /	...... / ......
....	...... /	...... /	...... /	...... /	...... /	...... / ......

.AEROBIC.

activity .... duration .... distance .... resistance .... calories

....

....

....

.RECOVERY/STRETCHES.

activity .... duration

....

....

....

....

....

.WATER.

. APPRECIATION .

.1...

.2...

.3...

W
E
E
K
•
1

M
T
W
T
F
S
S

.FOOD.

Meal 1:

....

....calories: ....

Meal 2:

....

....calories: ....

Meal 3:

....

....calories: ....

Meal 4:

....

....calories: ....

Meal 5:

....

....calories: ....

Meal 6:

....

....calories: ....

....total calories: ....

. W E I G H T • T R A I N I N G .

exercise	set 1	set 2	set 3	set 4	set 5	set 6
....	...... /	...... /	...... /	...... /	...... /	...... / ......
....	...... /	...... /	...... /	...... /	...... /	...... / ......
....	...... /	...... /	...... /	...... /	...... /	...... / ......
....	...... /	...... /	...... /	...... /	...... /	...... / ......
....	...... /	...... /	...... /	...... /	...... /	...... / ......
....	...... /	...... /	...... /	...... /	...... /	...... / ......
....	...... /	...... /	...... /	...... /	...... /	...... / ......
....	...... /	...... /	...... /	...... /	...... /	...... / ......
....	...... /	...... /	...... /	...... /	...... /	...... / ......
....	...... /	...... /	...... /	...... /	...... /	...... / ......

. A E R O B I C .

activity .... duration .... distance .... resistance .... calories

....

....

....

. R E C O V E R Y / S T R E T C H E S .

activity .... duration

....

....

....

....

....

. W A T E R .

. APPRECIATION .

.1...

.2...

.3...

W
E
E
K
•
1

M
T
W
T
F
S
S

. FOOD .

Meal 1:

....

....calories: ....

Meal 2:

....

....calories: ....

Meal 3:

....

....calories: ....

Meal 4:

....

....calories: ....

Meal 5:

....

....calories: ....

Meal 6:

....

....calories: ....

....total calories: ....

.WEIGHT•TRAINING.

exercise	set 1	set 2	set 3	set 4	set 5	set 6
....	...... /	...... /	...... /	...... /	...... /	...... / ......
....	...... /	...... /	...... /	...... /	...... /	...... / ......
....	...... /	...... /	...... /	...... /	...... /	...... / ......
....	...... /	...... /	...... /	...... /	...... /	...... / ......
....	...... /	...... /	...... /	...... /	...... /	...... / ......
....	...... /	...... /	...... /	...... /	...... /	...... / ......
....	...... /	...... /	...... /	...... /	...... /	...... / ......
....	...... /	...... /	...... /	...... /	...... /	...... / ......
....	...... /	...... /	...... /	...... /	...... /	...... / ......
....	...... /	...... /	...... /	...... /	...... /	...... / ......

.AEROBIC.

activity .... duration .... distance .... resistance .... calories

....

....

....

.RECOVERY/STRETCHES.

activity .... duration

....

....

....

....

....

.WATER.

. APPRECIATION .

.1..

.2..

.3..

W
E
E
K
•
1

M
T
W
T
F
S
S

.FOOD.

Meal 1:

....

....calories: ....

Meal 2:

....

....calories: ....

Meal 3:

....

....calories: ....

Meal 4:

....

....calories: ....

Meal 5:

....

....calories: ....

Meal 6:

....

....calories: ....

....total calories: ....

.WEIGHT•TRAINING.

exercise ...... set 1 ...... set 2 ...... set 3 ...... set 4 ...... set 5 ...... set 6

.... / .... / .... / .... / .... / .... / ......

.... / .... / .... / .... / .... / .... / ......

.... / .... / .... / .... / .... / .... / ......

.... / .... / .... / .... / .... / .... / ......

.... / .... / .... / .... / .... / .... / ......

.... / .... / .... / .... / .... / .... / ......

.... / .... / .... / .... / .... / .... / ......

.... / .... / .... / .... / .... / .... / ......

.... / .... / .... / .... / .... / .... / ......

.... / .... / .... / .... / .... / .... / ......

.AEROBIC.

activity .... duration .... distance .... resistance .... calories

....

....

....

.RECOVERY/STRETCHES.

activity .... duration

....

....

....

....

....

.WATER.

. APPRECIATION .

.1...

.2...

.3...

W
E
E
K
•
1

M
T
W
T
F
S
S

.FOOD.

Meal 1:

....

....calories: ....

Meal 2:

....

....calories: ....

Meal 3:

....

....calories: ....

Meal 4:

....

....calories: ....

Meal 5:

....

....calories: ....

Meal 6:

....

....calories: ....

....total calories: ....

.WEIGHT•TRAINING.

exercise	set 1	set 2	set 3	set 4	set 5	set 6
......	...... /	...... /	...... /	...... /	...... /	...... / ......
......	...... /	...... /	...... /	...... /	...... /	...... / ......
......	...... /	...... /	...... /	...... /	...... /	...... / ......
......	...... /	...... /	...... /	...... /	...... /	...... / ......
......	...... /	...... /	...... /	...... /	...... /	...... / ......
......	...... /	...... /	...... /	...... /	...... /	...... / ......
......	...... /	...... /	...... /	...... /	...... /	...... / ......
......	...... /	...... /	...... /	...... /	...... /	...... / ......
......	...... /	...... /	...... /	...... /	...... /	...... / ......
......	...... /	...... /	...... /	...... /	...... /	...... / ......

.AEROBIC.

activity .... duration .... distance .... resistance .... calories

....

....

....

.RECOVERY/STRETCHES.

activity .... duration

....

....

....

....

....

.WATER.

. A P P R E C I A T I O N .

.1..

.2..

.3..

W
E
E   ## . F O O D .
K
        ### Meal 1:
K
....
•
....calories: ....

1   ### Meal 2:

....

....calories: ....

        ### Meal 3:

M
....
T
....calories: ....

W   ### Meal 4:

T
....

....calories: ....
F
        ### Meal 5:
S
....
S
....calories: ....

        ### Meal 6:

....

....calories: ....

....total calories: ....

. W E I G H T • T R A I N I N G.

exercise	set 1	set 2	set 3	set 4	set 5	set 6
....	...... /	...... /	...... /	...... /	...... /	...... / ......
....	...... /	...... /	...... /	...... /	...... /	...... / ......
....	...... /	...... /	...... /	...... /	...... /	...... / ......
....	...... /	...... /	...... /	...... /	...... /	...... / ......
....	...... /	...... /	...... /	...... /	...... /	...... / ......
....	...... /	...... /	...... /	...... /	...... /	...... / ......
....	...... /	...... /	...... /	...... /	...... /	...... / ......
....	...... /	...... /	...... /	...... /	...... /	...... / ......
....	...... /	...... /	...... /	...... /	...... /	...... / ......
....	...... /	...... /	...... /	...... /	...... /	...... / ......

. A E R O B I C .

activity .... duration .... distance .... resistance .... calories

....

....

....

. R E C O V E R Y / S T R E T C H E S .

activity .... duration

....

....

....

....

....

. W A T E R .

WEEK. 7

Two roads diverged in the woods, and I took the one less traveled. That has made all the difference.

Goals:

....

....

....

....

....

Measurements:

.... Chest   Waist ....

.... Umbilicus   Hips ....

.... Right Bicep   Left Bicep ....

.... Right Thigh   Left Thigh ....

.... Right Calf   Left Calf ....

.... Weight   Body Fat ....

Progress Picture: []

This weeks Inspiration:

....

....

....

....

....

. Training Schedule .

Monday:

am ....

pm ....

Tuesday:

am ....

pm ....

Wednesday:

am ....

pm ....

Thursday:

am ....

pm ....

Friday:

am ....

pm ....

Saturday:

am ....

pm ....

Sunday

am ....

pm ....

. APPRECIATION .

.1...

.2...

.3...

W
E
E   # .FOOD.
K   ### Meal 1:

....

....calories: ....

           ### Meal 2:

....

....calories: ....

           ### Meal 3:

M
....

T
....calories: ....

W   ### Meal 4:

T
....

....calories: ....

F   ### Meal 5:

S
....

S
....calories: ....

           ### Meal 6:

....

....calories: ....

....total calories: ....

. W E I G H T • T R A I N I N G .

exercise ...... set 1 ...... set 2 ...... set 3 ...... set 4 ...... set 5 ...... set 6

.... / .... / .... / .... / .... / .... / ......

.... / .... / .... / .... / .... / .... / ......

.... / .... / .... / .... / .... / .... / ......

.... / .... / .... / .... / .... / .... / ......

.... / .... / .... / .... / .... / .... / ......

.... / .... / .... / .... / .... / .... / ......

.... / .... / .... / .... / .... / .... / ......

.... / .... / .... / .... / .... / .... / ......

.... / .... / .... / .... / .... / .... / ......

.... / .... / .... / .... / .... / .... / ......

. A E R O B I C .

activity .... duration .... distance .... resistance .... calories

....

....

....

. R E C O V E R Y / S T R E T C H E S .

activity .... duration

....

....

....

....

....

. W A T E R .

. A P P R E C I A T I O N .

.1...

.2...

.3...

W
E
E
K
•
1

M
T
W
T
F
S
S

. F O O D .

Meal 1:

....

....calories: ....

Meal 2:

....

....calories: ....

Meal 3:

....

....calories: ....

Meal 4:

....

....calories: ....

Meal 5:

....

....calories: ....

Meal 6:

....

....calories: ....

....total calories: ....

. W E I G H T • T R A I N I N G .

exercise	set 1	set 2	set 3	set 4	set 5	set 6
......	...... /	...... /	...... /	...... /	...... /	...... / ......
......	...... /	...... /	...... /	...... /	...... /	...... / ......
......	...... /	...... /	...... /	...... /	...... /	...... / ......
......	...... /	...... /	...... /	...... /	...... /	...... / ......
......	...... /	...... /	...... /	...... /	...... /	...... / ......
......	...... /	...... /	...... /	...... /	...... /	...... / ......
......	...... /	...... /	...... /	...... /	...... /	...... / ......
......	...... /	...... /	...... /	...... /	...... /	...... / ......
......	...... /	...... /	...... /	...... /	...... /	...... / ......
......	...... /	...... /	...... /	...... /	...... /	...... / ......

. A E R O B I C .

activity .... duration .... distance .... resistance .... calories

....

....

....

. R E C O V E R Y / S T R E T C H E S .

activity .... duration

....

....

....

....

....

. W A T E R .

. APPRECIATION.

.1..

.2..

.3..

W
E
E
K

·

1

M
T
W
T
F
S
S

.FOOD.

Meal 1:

....

....calories: ....

Meal 2:

....

....calories: ....

Meal 3:

....

....calories: ....

Meal 4:

....

....calories: ....

Meal 5:

....

....calories: ....

Meal 6:

....

....calories: ....

....total calories: ....

.WEIGHT•TRAINING.

exercise	set 1	set 2	set 3	set 4	set 5	set 6
....	...... /	...... /	...... /	...... /	...... /	...... / ......
....	...... /	...... /	...... /	...... /	...... /	...... / ......
....	...... /	...... /	...... /	...... /	...... /	...... / ......
....	...... /	...... /	...... /	...... /	...... /	...... / ......
....	...... /	...... /	...... /	...... /	...... /	...... / ......
....	...... /	...... /	...... /	...... /	...... /	...... / ......
....	...... /	...... /	...... /	...... /	...... /	...... / ......
....	...... /	...... /	...... /	...... /	...... /	...... / ......
....	...... /	...... /	...... /	...... /	...... /	...... / ......
....	...... /	...... /	...... /	...... /	...... /	...... / ......

.AEROBIC.

activity .... duration .... distance .... resistance .... calories

....

....

....

.RECOVERY/STRETCHES.

activity .... duration

....

....

....

....

....

.WATER.

. APPRECIATION .

.1...

.2...

.3...

W
E
E
K
•
1

M
T
W
T
F
S
S

.FOOD.

Meal 1:

....

....calories: ....

Meal 2:

....

....calories: ....

Meal 3:

....

....calories: ....

Meal 4:

....

....calories: ....

Meal 5:

....

....calories: ....

Meal 6:

....

....calories: ....

....total calories: ....

.WEIGHT•TRAINING.

exercise	set 1	set 2	set 3	set 4	set 5	set 6
....	...... /	...... /	...... /	...... /	...... /	...... / ......
....	...... /	...... /	...... /	...... /	...... /	...... / ......
....	...... /	...... /	...... /	...... /	...... /	...... / ......
....	...... /	...... /	...... /	...... /	...... /	...... / ......
....	...... /	...... /	...... /	...... /	...... /	...... / ......
....	...... /	...... /	...... /	...... /	...... /	...... / ......
....	...... /	...... /	...... /	...... /	...... /	...... / ......
....	...... /	...... /	...... /	...... /	...... /	...... / ......
....	...... /	...... /	...... /	...... /	...... /	...... / ......
....	...... /	...... /	...... /	...... /	...... /	...... / ......

.AEROBIC.

activity .... duration .... distance .... resistance .... calories

....

....

....

.RECOVERY/STRETCHES.

activity .... duration

....

....

....

....

....

.WATER.

. APPRECIATION .

.1...

.2...

.3...

W
E
E
K
•
1

M
T
W
T
F
S
S

.FOOD.
Meal 1:

....

....calories: ....

Meal 2:

....

....calories: ....

Meal 3:

....

....calories: ....

Meal 4:

....

....calories: ....

Meal 5:

....

....calories: ....

Meal 6:

....

....calories: ....

....total calories: ....

. W E I G H T · T R A I N I N G .

exercise	set 1	set 2	set 3	set 4	set 5	set 6
....	...... /	...... /	...... /	...... /	...... /	...... / ......
....	...... /	...... /	...... /	...... /	...... /	...... / ......
....	...... /	...... /	...... /	...... /	...... /	...... / ......
....	...... /	...... /	...... /	...... /	...... /	...... / ......
....	...... /	...... /	...... /	...... /	...... /	...... / ......
....	...... /	...... /	...... /	...... /	...... /	...... / ......
....	...... /	...... /	...... /	...... /	...... /	...... / ......
....	...... /	...... /	...... /	...... /	...... /	...... / ......
....	...... /	...... /	...... /	...... /	...... /	...... / ......
....	...... /	...... /	...... /	...... /	...... /	...... / ......

. A E R O B I C .

activity .... duration .... distance .... resistance .... calories

....

....

....

. R E C O V E R Y / S T R E T C H E S .

activity .... duration

....

....

....

....

....

. W A T E R .

. APPRECIATION .

.1..

.2..

.3..

W
E

.FOOD.

E
Meal 1:

K
....

....calories: ....

•
Meal 2:

1
....

....calories: ....

Meal 3:

M
....

T
....calories: ....

W
Meal 4:

T
....

....calories: ....

F
Meal 5:

S
....

S
....calories: ....

Meal 6:

....

....calories: ....

....total calories: ....

.WEIGHT•TRAINING.

exercise	set 1	set 2	set 3	set 4	set 5	set 6
....	...... /	...... /	...... /	...... /	...... /	...... / ......
....	...... /	...... /	...... /	...... /	...... /	...... / ......
....	...... /	...... /	...... /	...... /	...... /	...... / ......
....	...... /	...... /	...... /	...... /	...... /	...... / ......
....	...... /	...... /	...... /	...... /	...... /	...... / ......
....	...... /	...... /	...... /	...... /	...... /	...... / ......
....	...... /	...... /	...... /	...... /	...... /	...... / ......
....	...... /	...... /	...... /	...... /	...... /	...... / ......
....	...... /	...... /	...... /	...... /	...... /	...... / ......
....	...... /	...... /	...... /	...... /	...... /	...... / ......

.AEROBIC.

activity .... duration .... distance .... resistance .... calories

....

....

....

.RECOVERY/STRETCHES.

activity .... duration

....

....

....

....

....

.WATER.

. APPRECIATION .

.1..

.2..

.3..

W
E
E
K
•
1

M
T
W
T
F
S
S

.FOOD.

Meal 1:

....

....calories: ....

Meal 2:

....

....calories: ....

Meal 3:

....

....calories: ....

Meal 4:

....

....calories: ....

Meal 5:

....

....calories: ....

Meal 6:

....

....calories: ....

....total calories: ....

.WEIGHT•TRAINING.

exercise	set 1	set 2	set 3	set 4	set 5	set 6
....	...... /	...... /	...... /	...... /	...... /	...... / ......
....	...... /	...... /	...... /	...... /	...... /	...... / ......
....	...... /	...... /	...... /	...... /	...... /	...... / ......
....	...... /	...... /	...... /	...... /	...... /	...... / ......
....	...... /	...... /	...... /	...... /	...... /	...... / ......
....	...... /	...... /	...... /	...... /	...... /	...... / ......
....	...... /	...... /	...... /	...... /	...... /	...... / ......
....	...... /	...... /	...... /	...... /	...... /	...... / ......
....	...... /	...... /	...... /	...... /	...... /	...... / ......
....	...... /	...... /	...... /	...... /	...... /	...... / ......

.AEROBIC.

activity .... duration .... distance .... resistance .... calories

....

....

....

.RECOVERY/STRETCHES.

activity .... duration

....

....

....

....

....

.WATER.

W E E K

.

8

Spend time with the people who make you happy.

Goals:

....

....

....

....

....

Measurements:

.... Chest   Waist ....

.... Umbilicus   Hips ....

.... Right Bicep   Left Bicep ....

.... Right Thigh   Left Thigh ....

.... Right Calf   Left Calf ....

.... Weight   Body Fat ....

Progress Picture: []

This weeks Inspiration:

....

....

....

....

....

. Training Schedule .

Monday:

am ....

pm ....

Tuesday:

am ....

pm ....

Wednesday:

am ....

pm ....

Thursday:

am ....

pm ....

Friday:

am ....

pm ....

Saturday:

am ....

pm ....

Sunday

am ....

pm ....

. APPRECIATION .

.1..

.2..

.3..

W
E
E
K
.
1

M
T
W
T
F
S
S

. FOOD .

Meal 1:

....

....calories: ....

Meal 2:

....

....calories: ....

Meal 3:

....

....calories: ....

Meal 4:

....

....calories: ....

Meal 5:

....

....calories: ....

Meal 6:

....

....calories: ....

....total calories: ....

.WEIGHT•TRAINING.

exercise	set 1	set 2	set 3	set 4	set 5	set 6
....	...... /	...... /	...... /	...... /	...... /	...... / ......
....	...... /	...... /	...... /	...... /	...... /	...... / ......
....	...... /	...... /	...... /	...... /	...... /	...... / ......
....	...... /	...... /	...... /	...... /	...... /	...... / ......
....	...... /	...... /	...... /	...... /	...... /	...... / ......
....	...... /	...... /	...... /	...... /	...... /	...... / ......
....	...... /	...... /	...... /	...... /	...... /	...... / ......
....	...... /	...... /	...... /	...... /	...... /	...... / ......
....	...... /	...... /	...... /	...... /	...... /	...... / ......
....	...... /	...... /	...... /	...... /	...... /	...... / ......

.AEROBIC.

activity .... duration .... distance .... resistance .... calories

....

....

....

.RECOVERY/STRETCHES.

activity .... duration

....

....

....

....

....

.WATER.

. APPRECIATION .

.1..

.2..

.3..

W
E
E
K
•
1

M
T
W
T
F
S
S

. F O O D .

Meal 1:

....

....calories: ....

Meal 2:

....

....calories: ....

Meal 3:

....

....calories: ....

Meal 4:

....

....calories: ....

Meal 5:

....

....calories: ....

Meal 6:

....

....calories: ....

....total calories: ....

.WEIGHT•TRAINING.

exercise ...... set 1 ...... set 2 ...... set 3 ...... set 4 ...... set 5 ...... set 6

.... / .... / .... / .... / .... / .... / ......

.... / .... / .... / .... / .... / .... / ......

.... / .... / .... / .... / .... / .... / ......

.... / .... / .... / .... / .... / .... / ......

.... / .... / .... / .... / .... / .... / ......

.... / .... / .... / .... / .... / .... / ......

.... / .... / .... / .... / .... / .... / ......

.... / .... / .... / .... / .... / .... / ......

.... / .... / .... / .... / .... / .... / ......

.... / .... / .... / .... / .... / .... / ......

.AEROBIC.

activity .... duration .... distance .... resistance .... calories

....

....

....

.RECOVERY/STRETCHES.

activity .... duration

....

....

....

....

....

.WATER.

. APPRECIATION .

.1...

.2...

.3...

W
E
E
K
•
1

M
T
W
T
F
S
S

. F O O D .

Meal 1:

....

....calories: ....

Meal 2:

....

....calories: ....

Meal 3:

....

....calories: ....

Meal 4:

....

....calories: ....

Meal 5:

....

....calories: ....

Meal 6:

....

....calories: ....

....total calories: ....

.WEIGHT•TRAINING.

exercise	set 1	set 2	set 3	set 4	set 5	set 6
....	...... /	...... /	...... /	...... /	...... /	...... / ......
....	...... /	...... /	...... /	...... /	...... /	...... / ......
....	...... /	...... /	...... /	...... /	...... /	...... / ......
....	...... /	...... /	...... /	...... /	...... /	...... / ......
....	...... /	...... /	...... /	...... /	...... /	...... / ......
....	...... /	...... /	...... /	...... /	...... /	...... / ......
....	...... /	...... /	...... /	...... /	...... /	...... / ......
....	...... /	...... /	...... /	...... /	...... /	...... / ......
....	...... /	...... /	...... /	...... /	...... /	...... / ......
....	...... /	...... /	...... /	...... /	...... /	...... / ......

.AEROBIC.

activity .... duration .... distance .... resistance .... calories

....

....

....

.RECOVERY/STRETCHES.

activity .... duration

....

....

....

....

....

.WATER.

. APPRECIATION .

.1..

.2..

.3..

W
E
E
K
•
1

M
T
W
T
F
S
S

. F O O D .

Meal 1:

....

....calories: ....

Meal 2:

....

....calories: ....

Meal 3:

....

....calories: ....

Meal 4:

....

....calories: ....

Meal 5:

....

....calories: ....

Meal 6:

....

....calories: ....

....total calories: ....

.WEIGHT•TRAINING.

exercise	set 1	set 2	set 3	set 4	set 5	set 6
......	...... /	...... /	...... /	...... /	...... /	...... / ......
......	...... /	...... /	...... /	...... /	...... /	...... / ......
......	...... /	...... /	...... /	...... /	...... /	...... / ......
......	...... /	...... /	...... /	...... /	...... /	...... / ......
......	...... /	...... /	...... /	...... /	...... /	...... / ......
......	...... /	...... /	...... /	...... /	...... /	...... / ......
......	...... /	...... /	...... /	...... /	...... /	...... / ......
......	...... /	...... /	...... /	...... /	...... /	...... / ......
......	...... /	...... /	...... /	...... /	...... /	...... / ......
......	...... /	...... /	...... /	...... /	...... /	...... / ......

.AEROBIC.

activity .... duration .... distance .... resistance .... calories

....
....
....

.RECOVERY/STRETCHES.

activity .... duration

....
....
....
....
....

.WATER.

. APPRECIATION .

.1...

.2...

.3...

W
E
E
K
·
1

M
T
W
T
F
S
S

.FOOD.

Meal 1:

....

....calories: ....

Meal 2:

....

....calories: ....

Meal 3:

....

....calories: ....

Meal 4:

....

....calories: ....

Meal 5:

....

....calories: ....

Meal 6:

....

....calories: ....

....total calories: ....

.WEIGHT•TRAINING.

exercise	set 1	set 2	set 3	set 4	set 5	set 6
......	...... /	...... /	...... /	...... /	...... /	...... / ......
......	...... /	...... /	...... /	...... /	...... /	...... / ......
......	...... /	...... /	...... /	...... /	...... /	...... / ......
......	...... /	...... /	...... /	...... /	...... /	...... / ......
......	...... /	...... /	...... /	...... /	...... /	...... / ......
......	...... /	...... /	...... /	...... /	...... /	...... / ......
......	...... /	...... /	...... /	...... /	...... /	...... / ......
......	...... /	...... /	...... /	...... /	...... /	...... / ......
......	...... /	...... /	...... /	...... /	...... /	...... / ......
......	...... /	...... /	...... /	...... /	...... /	...... / ......

.AEROBIC.

activity .... duration .... distance .... resistance .... calories

....

....

....

.RECOVERY/STRETCHES.

activity .... duration

....

....

....

....

....

.WATER.

. A P P R E C I A T I O N .

.1..

.2..

.3..

W
E
E
K
•
1

M
T
W
T
F
S
S

. F O O D .

Meal 1:

....

....calories: ....

Meal 2:

....

....calories: ....

Meal 3:

....

....calories: ....

Meal 4:

....

....calories: ....

Meal 5:

....

....calories: ....

Meal 6:

....

....calories: ....

....total calories: ....

.WEIGHT•TRAINING.

exercise	set 1	set 2	set 3	set 4	set 5	set 6
....	...... /	...... /	...... /	...... /	...... /	...... / ......
....	...... /	...... /	...... /	...... /	...... /	...... / ......
....	...... /	...... /	...... /	...... /	...... /	...... / ......
....	...... /	...... /	...... /	...... /	...... /	...... / ......
....	...... /	...... /	...... /	...... /	...... /	...... / ......
....	...... /	...... /	...... /	...... /	...... /	...... / ......
....	...... /	...... /	...... /	...... /	...... /	...... / ......
....	...... /	...... /	...... /	...... /	...... /	...... / ......
....	...... /	...... /	...... /	...... /	...... /	...... / ......
....	...... /	...... /	...... /	...... /	...... /	...... / ......

.AEROBIC.

activity .... duration .... distance .... resistance .... calories

....

....

....

.RECOVERY/STRETCHES.

activity .... duration

....

....

....

....

....

.WATER.

. APPRECIATION .

.1...

.2...

.3...

W
E
E
K
•
1

.FOOD.

Meal 1:

....

....calories: ....

Meal 2:

....

....calories: ....

Meal 3:

....

....calories: ....

Meal 4:

....

....calories: ....

Meal 5:

....

....calories: ....

Meal 6:

....

....calories: ....

....total calories: ....

M
T
W
T
F
S
S

.WEIGHT•TRAINING.

exercise	set 1	set 2	set 3	set 4	set 5	set 6
....	...... /	...... /	...... /	...... /	...... /	...... / ......
....	...... /	...... /	...... /	...... /	...... /	...... / ......
....	...... /	...... /	...... /	...... /	...... /	...... / ......
....	...... /	...... /	...... /	...... /	...... /	...... / ......
....	...... /	...... /	...... /	...... /	...... /	...... / ......
....	...... /	...... /	...... /	...... /	...... /	...... / ......
....	...... /	...... /	...... /	...... /	...... /	...... / ......
....	...... /	...... /	...... /	...... /	...... /	...... / ......
....	...... /	...... /	...... /	...... /	...... /	...... / ......
....	...... /	...... /	...... /	...... /	...... /	...... / ......

.AEROBIC.

activity .... duration .... distance .... resistance .... calories

....

....

....

.RECOVERY/STRETCHES.

activity .... duration

....

....

....

....

....

.WATER.

W E E K · 9

Look at
the stars.
Look how
they shine
for you.

Goals:

....

....

....

....

....

Measurements:

.... Chest	Waist ....
.... Umbilicus	Hips ....
.... Right Bicep	Left Bicep ....
.... Right Thigh	Left Thigh ....
.... Right Calf	Left Calf ....
.... Weight	Body Fat ....

Progress Picture: []

This weeks Inspiration:

....

....

....

....

....

. Training Schedule .

Monday:

am ....

pm ....

Tuesday:

am ....

pm ....

Wednesday:

am ....

pm ....

Thursday:

am ....

pm ....

Friday:

am ....

pm ....

Saturday:

am ....

pm ....

Sunday

am ....

pm ....

. APPRECIATION.

.1..

.2..

.3..

W
E
E
K
•
1

M
T
W
T
F
S
S

.FOOD.

Meal 1:

....

....calories: ....

Meal 2:

....

....calories: ....

Meal 3:

....

....calories: ....

Meal 4:

....

....calories: ....

Meal 5:

....

....calories: ....

Meal 6:

....

....calories: ....

....total calories: ....

.WEIGHT•TRAINING.

exercise	set 1	set 2	set 3	set 4	set 5	set 6
....	...... /	...... /	...... /	...... /	...... /	...... / ......
....	...... /	...... /	...... /	...... /	...... /	...... / ......
....	...... /	...... /	...... /	...... /	...... /	...... / ......
....	...... /	...... /	...... /	...... /	...... /	...... / ......
....	...... /	...... /	...... /	...... /	...... /	...... / ......
....	...... /	...... /	...... /	...... /	...... /	...... / ......
....	...... /	...... /	...... /	...... /	...... /	...... / ......
....	...... /	...... /	...... /	...... /	...... /	...... / ......
....	...... /	...... /	...... /	...... /	...... /	...... / ......
....	...... /	...... /	...... /	...... /	...... /	...... / ......

.AEROBIC.

activity .... duration .... distance .... resistance .... calories

....

....

....

.RECOVERY/STRETCHES.

activity .... duration

....

....

....

....

....

.WATER.

. A P P R E C I A T I O N .

.1..

.2..

.3..

W
E
E
K
•
1

M
T
W
T
F
S
S

. F O O D .

Meal 1:

....

....calories: ....

Meal 2:

....

....calories: ....

Meal 3:

....

....calories: ....

Meal 4:

....

....calories: ....

Meal 5:

....

....calories: ....

Meal 6:

....

....calories: ....

....total calories: ....

.WEIGHT•TRAINING.

exercise	set 1	set 2	set 3	set 4	set 5	set 6
....	..../....	..../....	..../....	..../....	..../....	..../....
....	..../....	..../....	..../....	..../....	..../....	..../....
....	..../....	..../....	..../....	..../....	..../....	..../....
....	..../....	..../....	..../....	..../....	..../....	..../....
....	..../....	..../....	..../....	..../....	..../....	..../....
....	..../....	..../....	..../....	..../....	..../....	..../....
....	..../....	..../....	..../....	..../....	..../....	..../....
....	..../....	..../....	..../....	..../....	..../....	..../....
....	..../....	..../....	..../....	..../....	..../....	..../....
....	..../....	..../....	..../....	..../....	..../....	..../....

.AEROBIC.

activity .... duration .... distance .... resistance .... calories

....
....
....

.RECOVERY/STRETCHES.

activity .... duration

....
....
....
....
....

.WATER.

. APPRECIATION .

.1...

.2...

.3...

W
E
E
K
.
1

M
T
W
T
F
S
S

.FOOD.

Meal 1:

....

....calories: ....

Meal 2:

....

....calories: ....

Meal 3:

....

....calories: ....

Meal 4:

....

....calories: ....

Meal 5:

....

....calories: ....

Meal 6:

....

....calories: ....

....total calories: ....

. W E I G H T • T R A I N I N G .

exercise	set 1	set 2	set 3	set 4	set 5	set 6
......	...... /	...... /	...... /	...... /	...... /	...... / ......
......	...... /	...... /	...... /	...... /	...... /	...... / ......
......	...... /	...... /	...... /	...... /	...... /	...... / ......
......	...... /	...... /	...... /	...... /	...... /	...... / ......
......	...... /	...... /	...... /	...... /	...... /	...... / ......
......	...... /	...... /	...... /	...... /	...... /	...... / ......
......	...... /	...... /	...... /	...... /	...... /	...... / ......
......	...... /	...... /	...... /	...... /	...... /	...... / ......
......	...... /	...... /	...... /	...... /	...... /	...... / ......
......	...... /	...... /	...... /	...... /	...... /	...... / ......

. A E R O B I C .

activity .... duration .... distance .... resistance .... calories

....

....

....

. R E C O V E R Y / S T R E T C H E S .

activity .... duration

....

....

....

....

....

. W A T E R .

. APPRECIATION.

.1...

.2...

.3...

W
E

.FOOD.

E

Meal 1:

K

....

.

....calories: ....

Meal 2:

1

....

....calories: ....

Meal 3:

M

....

T

....calories: ....

W

Meal 4:

T

....

....calories: ....

F

Meal 5:

S

....

S

....calories: ....

Meal 6:

....

....calories: ....

....total calories: ....

.WEIGHT•TRAINING.

exercise	set 1	set 2	set 3	set 4	set 5	set 6
....	..... /	..... /	..... /	..... /	..... /	..... / .....
....	..... /	..... /	..... /	..... /	..... /	..... / .....
....	..... /	..... /	..... /	..... /	..... /	..... / .....
....	..... /	..... /	..... /	..... /	..... /	..... / .....
....	..... /	..... /	..... /	..... /	..... /	..... / .....
....	..... /	..... /	..... /	..... /	..... /	..... / .....
....	..... /	..... /	..... /	..... /	..... /	..... / .....
....	..... /	..... /	..... /	..... /	..... /	..... / .....
....	..... /	..... /	..... /	..... /	..... /	..... / .....
....	..... /	..... /	..... /	..... /	..... /	..... / .....

.AEROBIC.

activity .... duration .... distance .... resistance .... calories

....

....

....

.RECOVERY/STRETCHES.

activity .... duration

....

....

....

....

....

.WATER.

. APPRECIATION .

.1...

.2...

.3...

W
E
E
K
•
1

M
T
W
T
F
S
S

. F O O D .

Meal 1:

....

....calories: ....

Meal 2:

....

....calories: ....

Meal 3:

....

....calories: ....

Meal 4:

....

....calories: ....

Meal 5:

....

....calories: ....

Meal 6:

....

....calories: ....

....total calories: ....

.WEIGHT·TRAINING.

exercise	set 1	set 2	set 3	set 4	set 5	set 6
....	...... /	...... /	...... /	...... /	...... /	...... / ......
....	...... /	...... /	...... /	...... /	...... /	...... / ......
....	...... /	...... /	...... /	...... /	...... /	...... / ......
....	...... /	...... /	...... /	...... /	...... /	...... / ......
....	...... /	...... /	...... /	...... /	...... /	...... / ......
....	...... /	...... /	...... /	...... /	...... /	...... / ......
....	...... /	...... /	...... /	...... /	...... /	...... / ......
....	...... /	...... /	...... /	...... /	...... /	...... / ......
....	...... /	...... /	...... /	...... /	...... /	...... / ......
....	...... /	...... /	...... /	...... /	...... /	...... / ......

.AEROBIC.

activity .... duration .... distance .... resistance .... calories

....

....

....

.RECOVERY/STRETCHES.

activity .... duration

....

....

....

....

....

.WATER.

. APPRECIATION .

.1..

.2..

.3..

W
E
E
K
.
1

M
T
W
T
F
S
S

.FOOD.

Meal 1:

....

....calories: ....

Meal 2:

....

....calories: ....

Meal 3:

....

....calories: ....

Meal 4:

....

....calories: ....

Meal 5:

....

....calories: ....

Meal 6:

....

....calories: ....

....total calories: ....

.WEIGHT•TRAINING.

exercise	set 1	set 2	set 3	set 4	set 5	set 6
....	...... /	...... /	...... /	...... /	...... /	...... / ......
....	...... /	...... /	...... /	...... /	...... /	...... / ......
....	...... /	...... /	...... /	...... /	...... /	...... / ......
....	...... /	...... /	...... /	...... /	...... /	...... / ......
....	...... /	...... /	...... /	...... /	...... /	...... / ......
....	...... /	...... /	...... /	...... /	...... /	...... / ......
....	...... /	...... /	...... /	...... /	...... /	...... / ......
....	...... /	...... /	...... /	...... /	...... /	...... / ......
....	...... /	...... /	...... /	...... /	...... /	...... / ......
....	...... /	...... /	...... /	...... /	...... /	...... / ......

.AEROBIC.

activity .... duration .... distance .... resistance .... calories

....

....

....

.RECOVERY/STRETCHES.

activity .... duration

....

....

....

....

....

.WATER.

. A P P R E C I A T I O N .

.1..

.2..

.3..

W
E
E
K
•
1

M
T
W
T
F
S
S

. F O O D .

Meal 1:

....

....calories: ....

Meal 2:

....

....calories: ....

Meal 3:

....

....calories: ....

Meal 4:

....

....calories: ....

Mcal 5:

....

....calories: ....

Meal 6:

....

....calories: ....

....total calories: ....

. W E I G H T • T R A I N I N G.

exercise	set 1	set 2	set 3	set 4	set 5	set 6
......	...... /	...... /	...... /	...... /	...... /	...... / ......
......	...... /	...... /	...... /	...... /	...... /	...... / ......
......	...... /	...... /	...... /	...... /	...... /	...... / ......
......	...... /	...... /	...... /	...... /	...... /	...... / ......
......	...... /	...... /	...... /	...... /	...... /	...... / ......
......	...... /	...... /	...... /	...... /	...... /	...... / ......
......	...... /	...... /	...... /	...... /	...... /	...... / ......
......	...... /	...... /	...... /	...... /	...... /	...... / ......
......	...... /	...... /	...... /	...... /	...... /	...... / ......
......	...... /	...... /	...... /	...... /	...... /	...... / ......

. A E R O B I C.

activity .... duration .... distance .... resistance .... calories

....
....
....

. R E C O V E R Y / S T R E T C H E S.

activity .... duration

....
....
....
....
....

. W A T E R.

WEEK.10

When you truly don't care what anyone thinks of you, you have reached a dangerously awesome level of freedom.

Goals:

....

....

....

....

....

Measurements:

.... Chest   Waist ....

.... Umbilicus   Hips ....

.... Right Bicep   Left Bicep ....

.... Right Thigh   Left Thigh ....

.... Right Calf   Left Calf ....

.... Weight   Body Fat ....

Progress Picture: []

This weeks Inspiration:

....

....

....

....

....

. Training Schedule .

Monday:

am ....

pm ....

Tuesday:

am ....

pm ....

Wednesday:

am ....

pm ....

Thursday:

am ....

pm ....

Friday:

am ....

pm ....

Saturday:

am ....

pm ....

Sunday

am ....

pm ....

. APPRECIATION .

.1...

.2...

.3...

W
E
E
K
•
1

M
T
W
T
F
S
S

. FOOD .

Meal 1:

....

....calories: ....

Meal 2:

....

....calories: ....

Meal 3:

....

....calories: ....

Meal 4:

....

....calories: ....

Meal 5:

....

....calories: ....

Meal 6:

....

....calories: ....

....total calories: ....

.WEIGHT•TRAINING.

exercise	set 1	set 2	set 3	set 4	set 5	set 6
....	...... /	...... /	...... /	...... /	...... /	...... / ......
....	...... /	...... /	...... /	...... /	...... /	...... / ......
....	...... /	...... /	...... /	...... /	...... /	...... / ......
....	...... /	...... /	...... /	...... /	...... /	...... / ......
....	...... /	...... /	...... /	...... /	...... /	...... / ......
....	...... /	...... /	...... /	...... /	...... /	...... / ......
....	...... /	...... /	...... /	...... /	...... /	...... / ......
....	...... /	...... /	...... /	...... /	...... /	...... / ......
....	...... /	...... /	...... /	...... /	...... /	...... / ......
....	...... /	...... /	...... /	...... /	...... /	...... / ......

.AEROBIC.

activity .... duration .... distance .... resistance .... calories

....

....

....

.RECOVERY/STRETCHES.

activity .... duration

....

....

....

....

....

.WATER.

. APPRECIATION.

.1..

.2..

.3..

W
E
E
K
.
1

M
T
W
T
F
S
S

.FOOD.

Meal 1:

....

....calories: ....

Meal 2:

....

....calories: ....

Meal 3:

....

....calories: ....

Meal 4:

....

....calories: ....

Meal 5:

....

....calories: ....

Meal 6:

....

....calories: ....

....total calories: ....

. W E I G H T • T R A I N I N G .

exercise	set 1	set 2	set 3	set 4	set 5	set 6
....	.... /	.... /	.... /	.... /	.... /	.... / ......
....	.... /	.... /	.... /	.... /	.... /	.... / ......
....	.... /	.... /	.... /	.... /	.... /	.... / ......
....	.... /	.... /	.... /	.... /	.... /	.... / ......
....	.... /	.... /	.... /	.... /	.... /	.... / ......
....	.... /	.... /	.... /	.... /	.... /	.... / ......
....	.... /	.... /	.... /	.... /	.... /	.... / ......
....	.... /	.... /	.... /	.... /	.... /	.... / ......
....	.... /	.... /	.... /	.... /	.... /	.... / ......
....	.... /	.... /	.... /	.... /	.... /	.... / ......

. A E R O B I C .

activity .... duration .... distance .... resistance .... calories

....

....

....

. R E C O V E R Y / S T R E T C H E S .

activity .... duration

....

....

....

....

....

. W A T E R .

. APPRECIATION .

.1...

.2...

.3...

W
E
E
K
•
1

M
T
W
T
F
S
S

.FOOD.

Meal 1:

....

....calories: ....

Meal 2:

....

....calories: ....

Meal 3:

....

....calories: ....

Meal 4:

....

....calories: ....

Meal 5:

....

....calories: ....

Meal 6:

....

....calories: ....

....total calories: ....

. W E I G H T · T R A I N I N G .

exercise	set 1	set 2	set 3	set 4	set 5	set 6
....	...... /	...... /	...... /	...... /	...... /	...... / ......
....	...... /	...... /	...... /	...... /	...... /	...... / ......
....	...... /	...... /	...... /	...... /	...... /	...... / ......
....	...... /	...... /	...... /	...... /	...... /	...... / ......
....	...... /	...... /	...... /	...... /	...... /	...... / ......
....	...... /	...... /	...... /	...... /	...... /	...... / ......
....	...... /	...... /	...... /	...... /	...... /	...... / ......
....	...... /	...... /	...... /	...... /	...... /	...... / ......
....	...... /	...... /	...... /	...... /	...... /	...... / ......
....	...... /	...... /	...... /	...... /	...... /	...... / ......

. A E R O B I C .

activity .... duration .... distance .... resistance .... calories

....

....

....

. R E C O V E R Y / S T R E T C H E S .

activity .... duration

....

....

....

....

....

. W A T E R .

. A P P R E C I A T I O N .

.1..

.2..

.3..

W
E
E
K
•
1

M
T
W
T
F
S
S

. F O O D .

Meal 1:

....

....calories: ....

Meal 2:

....

....calories: ....

Meal 3:

....

....calories: ....

Meal 4:

....

....calories: ....

Meal 5:

....

....calories: ....

Meal 6:

....

....calories: ....

....total calories: ....

. W E I G H T • T R A I N I N G .

exercise	set 1	set 2	set 3	set 4	set 5	set 6
......	...... /	...... /	...... /	...... /	...... /	...... / ......
......	...... /	...... /	...... /	...... /	...... /	...... / ......
......	...... /	...... /	...... /	...... /	...... /	...... / ......
......	...... /	...... /	...... /	...... /	...... /	...... / ......
......	...... /	...... /	...... /	...... /	...... /	...... / ......
......	...... /	...... /	...... /	...... /	...... /	...... / ......
......	...... /	...... /	...... /	...... /	...... /	...... / ......
......	...... /	...... /	...... /	...... /	...... /	...... / ......
......	...... /	...... /	...... /	...... /	...... /	...... / ......
......	...... /	...... /	...... /	...... /	...... /	...... / ......

. A E R O B I C .

activity .... duration .... distance .... resistance .... calories

....

....

....

. R E C O V E R Y / S T R E T C H E S .

activity .... duration

....

....

....

....

....

. W A T E R .

. APPRECIATION .

.1..

.2..

.3..

W
E
E
K
•
1

M
T
W
T
F
S
S

. F O O D .

Meal 1:

....

....calories: ....

Meal 2:

....

....calories: ....

Meal 3:

....

....calories: ....

Meal 4:

....

....calories: ....

Meal 5:

....

....calories: ....

Meal 6:

....

....calories: ....

....total calories: ....

.WEIGHT•TRAINING.

exercise	set 1	set 2	set 3	set 4	set 5	set 6
....	...... /	...... /	...... /	...... /	...... /	...... / ......
....	...... /	...... /	...... /	...... /	...... /	...... / ......
....	...... /	...... /	...... /	...... /	...... /	...... / ......
....	...... /	...... /	...... /	...... /	...... /	...... / ......
....	...... /	...... /	...... /	...... /	...... /	...... / ......
....	...... /	...... /	...... /	...... /	...... /	...... / ......
....	...... /	...... /	...... /	...... /	...... /	...... / ......
....	...... /	...... /	...... /	...... /	...... /	...... / ......
....	...... /	...... /	...... /	...... /	...... /	...... / ......
....	...... /	...... /	...... /	...... /	...... /	...... / ......

.AEROBIC.

activity .... duration .... distance .... resistance .... calories

....
....
....

.RECOVERY/STRETCHES.

activity .... duration

....
....
....
....
....

.WATER.

. APPRECIATION .

.1..

.2..

.3..

W
E
E
K
•
1

M
T
W
T
F
S
S

. F O O D .

Meal 1:

....

....calories: ....

Meal 2:

....

....calories: ....

Meal 3:

....

....calories: ....

Meal 4:

....

....calories: ....

Meal 5:

....

....calories: ....

Meal 6:

....

....calories: ....

....total calories: ....

. W E I G H T • T R A I N I N G .

exercise	set 1	set 2	set 3	set 4	set 5	set 6
......	...... /	...... /	...... /	...... /	...... /	...... / ......
......	...... /	...... /	...... /	...... /	...... /	...... / ......
......	...... /	...... /	...... /	...... /	...... /	...... / ......
......	...... /	...... /	...... /	...... /	...... /	...... / ......
......	...... /	...... /	...... /	...... /	...... /	...... / ......
......	...... /	...... /	...... /	...... /	...... /	...... / ......
......	...... /	...... /	...... /	...... /	...... /	...... / ......
......	...... /	...... /	...... /	...... /	...... /	...... / ......
......	...... /	...... /	...... /	...... /	...... /	...... / ......
......	...... /	...... /	...... /	...... /	...... /	...... / ......

. A E R O B I C .

activity .... duration .... distance .... resistance .... calories

....

....

....

. R E C O V E R Y / S T R E T C H E S .

activity .... duration

....

....

....

....

....

. W A T E R .

. APPRECIATION .

.1..

.2..

.3..

W
E
E
K
•
1

M
T
W
T
F
S
S

. FOOD .

Meal 1:

....

....calories: ....

Meal 2:

....

....calories: ....

Meal 3:

....

....calories: ....

Meal 4:

....

....calories: ....

Meal 5:

....

....calories: ....

Meal 6:

....

....calories: ....

....total calories: ....

.WEIGHT•TRAINING.

exercise	set 1	set 2	set 3	set 4	set 5	set 6
....	...... /	...... /	...... /	...... /	...... /	...... / ......
....	...... /	...... /	...... /	...... /	...... /	...... / ......
....	...... /	...... /	...... /	...... /	...... /	...... / ......
....	...... /	...... /	...... /	...... /	...... /	...... / ......
....	...... /	...... /	...... /	...... /	...... /	...... / ......
....	...... /	...... /	...... /	...... /	...... /	...... / ......
....	...... /	...... /	...... /	...... /	...... /	...... / ......
....	...... /	...... /	...... /	...... /	...... /	...... / ......
....	...... /	...... /	...... /	...... /	...... /	...... / ......
....	...... /	...... /	...... /	...... /	...... /	...... / ......

.AEROBIC.

activity .... duration .... distance .... resistance .... calories

....
....
....

.RECOVERY/STRETCHES.

activity .... duration

....
....
....
....
....

.WATER.

WEEK

11

Be yourself; everyone else is taken.

Goals:

....

....

....

....

....

Measurements:

.... Chest   Waist ....

.... Umbilicus   Hips ....

.... Right Bicep   Left Bicep ....

.... Right Thigh   Left Thigh ....

.... Right Calf   Left Calf ....

.... Weight   Body Fat ....

Progress Picture: []

This weeks Inspiration:

....

....

....

....

....

. Training Schedule .

Monday:

am ....

pm ....

Tuesday:

am ....

pm ....

Wednesday:

am ....

pm ....

Thursday:

am ....

pm ....

Friday:

am ....

pm ....

Saturday:

am ....

pm ....

Sunday

am ....

pm ....

. APPRECIATION .

.1..

.2..

.3..

W
E
E
K
•
1

M
T
W
T
F
S
S

.FOOD.

Meal 1:

....

....calories: ....

Meal 2:

....

....calories: ....

Meal 3:

....

....calories: ....

Meal 4:

....

....calories: ....

Meal 5:

....

....calories: ....

Meal 6:

....

....calories: ....

....total calories: ....

.WEIGHT•TRAINING.

exercise	set 1	set 2	set 3	set 4	set 5	set 6
......	...... /	...... /	...... /	...... /	...... /	...... / ......
......	...... /	...... /	...... /	...... /	...... /	...... / ......
......	...... /	...... /	...... /	...... /	...... /	...... / ......
......	...... /	...... /	...... /	...... /	...... /	...... / ......
......	...... /	...... /	...... /	...... /	...... /	...... / ......
......	...... /	...... /	...... /	...... /	...... /	...... / ......
......	...... /	...... /	...... /	...... /	...... /	...... / ......
......	...... /	...... /	...... /	...... /	...... /	...... / ......
......	...... /	...... /	...... /	...... /	...... /	...... / ......
......	...... /	...... /	...... /	...... /	...... /	...... / ......

.AEROBIC.

activity .... duration .... distance .... resistance .... calories

....

....

....

.RECOVERY/STRETCHES.

activity .... duration

....

....

....

....

....

.WATER.

. APPRECIATION .

.1..

.2..

.3..

W
E
E
K
•
1

M
T
W
T
F
S
S

. F O O D .

Meal 1:

....

....calories: ....

Meal 2:

....

....calories: ....

Meal 3:

....

....calories: ....

Meal 4:

....

....calories: ....

Meal 5:

....

....calories: ....

Meal 6:

....

....calories: ....

....total calories: ....

.WEIGHT•TRAINING.

exercise	set 1	set 2	set 3	set 4	set 5	set 6
....	...... /	...... /	...... /	...... /	...... /	...... / ......
....	...... /	...... /	...... /	...... /	...... /	...... / ......
....	...... /	...... /	...... /	...... /	...... /	...... / ......
....	...... /	...... /	...... /	...... /	...... /	...... / ......
....	...... /	...... /	...... /	...... /	...... /	...... / ......
....	...... /	...... /	...... /	...... /	...... /	...... / ......
....	...... /	...... /	...... /	...... /	...... /	...... / ......
....	...... /	...... /	...... /	...... /	...... /	...... / ......
....	...... /	...... /	...... /	...... /	...... /	...... / ......
....	...... /	...... /	...... /	...... /	...... /	...... / ......

.AEROBIC.

activity .... duration .... distance .... resistance .... calories

....

....

....

.RECOVERY/STRETCHES.

activity .... duration

....

....

....

....

....

.WATER.

. APPRECIATION .

.1..

.2..

.3..

W

E

E
. F O O D .

K
Meal 1:

•
....

1
....calories: ....

Meal 2:

....

....calories: ....

M
Meal 3:

....

T
....calories: ....

W
Meal 4:

....

T
....calories: ....

F
Meal 5:

S
....

S
....calories: ....

Meal 6:

....

....calories: ....

....total calories: ....

.WEIGHT•TRAINING.

exercise	set 1	set 2	set 3	set 4	set 5	set 6
....	..... /	..... /	..... /	..... /	..... /	..... / .....
....	..... /	..... /	..... /	..... /	..... /	..... / .....
....	..... /	..... /	..... /	..... /	..... /	..... / .....
....	..... /	..... /	..... /	..... /	..... /	..... / .....
....	..... /	..... /	..... /	..... /	..... /	..... / .....
....	..... /	..... /	..... /	..... /	..... /	..... / .....
....	..... /	..... /	..... /	..... /	..... /	..... / .....
....	..... /	..... /	..... /	..... /	..... /	..... / .....
....	..... /	..... /	..... /	..... /	..... /	..... / .....
....	..... /	..... /	..... /	..... /	..... /	..... / .....

.AEROBIC.

activity .... duration .... distance .... resistance .... calories

....

....

....

.RECOVERY/STRETCHES.

activity .... duration

....

....

....

....

....

.WATER.

. APPRECIATION .

.1..

.2..

.3..

W
E
E
K
•
1

M
T
W
T
F
S
S

.FOOD.

Meal 1:

....

....calories: ....

Meal 2:

....

....calories: ....

Meal 3:

....

....calories: ....

Meal 4:

....

....calories: ....

Meal 5:

....

....calories: ....

Meal 6:

....

....calories: ....

....total calories: ....

.WEIGHT•TRAINING.

exercise	set 1	set 2	set 3	set 4	set 5	set 6
....	...... /	...... /	...... /	...... /	...... /	...... / ......
....	...... /	...... /	...... /	...... /	...... /	...... / ......
....	...... /	...... /	...... /	...... /	...... /	...... / ......
....	...... /	...... /	...... /	...... /	...... /	...... / ......
....	...... /	...... /	...... /	...... /	...... /	...... / ......
....	...... /	...... /	...... /	...... /	...... /	...... / ......
....	...... /	...... /	...... /	...... /	...... /	...... / ......
....	...... /	...... /	...... /	...... /	...... /	...... / ......
....	...... /	...... /	...... /	...... /	...... /	...... / ......
....	...... /	...... /	...... /	...... /	...... /	...... / ......

.AEROBIC.

activity .... duration .... distance .... resistance .... calories

....

....

....

.RECOVERY/STRETCHES.

activity .... duration

....

....

....

....

....

.WATER.

. APPRECIATION .

.1...

.2...

.3...

W
E
E
K
•
1

M
T
W
T
F
S
S

. F O O D .

Meal 1:

....

....calories: ....

Meal 2:

....

....calories: ....

Meal 3:

....

....calories: ....

Meal 4:

....

....calories: ....

Meal 5:

....

....calories: ....

Meal 6:

....

....calories: ....

....total calories: ....

. W E I G H T • T R A I N I N G .

exercise	set 1	set 2	set 3	set 4	set 5	set 6
....	...... /	...... /	...... /	...... /	...... /	...... / ......
....	...... /	...... /	...... /	...... /	...... /	...... / ......
....	...... /	...... /	...... /	...... /	...... /	...... / ......
....	...... /	...... /	...... /	...... /	...... /	...... / ......
....	...... /	...... /	...... /	...... /	...... /	...... / ......
....	...... /	...... /	...... /	...... /	...... /	...... / ......
....	...... /	...... /	...... /	...... /	...... /	...... / ......
....	...... /	...... /	...... /	...... /	...... /	...... / ......
....	...... /	...... /	...... /	...... /	...... /	...... / ......
....	...... /	...... /	...... /	...... /	...... /	...... / ......

. A E R O B I C .

activity .... duration .... distance .... resistance .... calories

....

....

....

. R E C O V E R Y / S T R E T C H E S .

activity .... duration

....

....

....

....

....

. W A T E R .

. APPRECIATION .

.1 ....

.2 ....

.3 ....

W
E
E
K

•

1

M
T
W
T
F
S
S

. FOOD .

Meal 1:

....

....calories: ....

Meal 2:

....

....calories: ....

Meal 3:

....

....calories: ....

Meal 4:

....

....calories: ....

Meal 5:

....

....calories: ....

Meal 6:

....

....calories: ....

....total calories: ....

.WEIGHT•TRAINING.

exercise	set 1	set 2	set 3	set 4	set 5	set 6
....	...... /	...... /	...... /	...... /	...... /	...... / ......
....	...... /	...... /	...... /	...... /	...... /	...... / ......
....	...... /	...... /	...... /	...... /	...... /	...... / ......
....	...... /	...... /	...... /	...... /	...... /	...... / ......
....	...... /	...... /	...... /	...... /	...... /	...... / ......
....	...... /	...... /	...... /	...... /	...... /	...... / ......
....	...... /	...... /	...... /	...... /	...... /	...... / ......
....	...... /	...... /	...... /	...... /	...... /	...... / ......
....	...... /	...... /	...... /	...... /	...... /	...... / ......
....	...... /	...... /	...... /	...... /	...... /	...... / ......

.AEROBIC.

activity .... duration .... distance .... resistance .... calories

....

....

....

.RECOVERY/STRETCHES.

activity .... duration

....

....

....

....

....

.WATER.

. A P P R E C I A T I O N .

.1..

.2..

.3..

W
E
E
K
•
1

M
T
W
T
F
S
S

. F O O D .

Meal 1:

....

....calories: ....

Meal 2:

....

....calories: ....

Meal 3:

....

....calories: ....

Meal 4:

....

....calories: ....

Meal 5:

....

....calories: ....

Meal 6:

....

....calories: ....

....total calories: ....

.WEIGHT•TRAINING.

exercise	set 1	set 2	set 3	set 4	set 5	set 6
......	...... /	...... /	...... /	...... /	...... /	...... / ......
......	...... /	...... /	...... /	...... /	...... /	...... / ......
......	...... /	...... /	...... /	...... /	...... /	...... / ......
......	...... /	...... /	...... /	...... /	...... /	...... / ......
......	...... /	...... /	...... /	...... /	...... /	...... / ......
......	...... /	...... /	...... /	...... /	...... /	...... / ......
......	...... /	...... /	...... /	...... /	...... /	...... / ......
......	...... /	...... /	...... /	...... /	...... /	...... / ......
......	...... /	...... /	...... /	...... /	...... /	...... / ......
......	...... /	...... /	...... /	...... /	...... /	...... / ......

.AEROBIC.

activity .... duration .... distance .... resistance .... calories

....

....

....

.RECOVERY/STRETCHES.

activity .... duration

....

....

....

....

....

.WATER.

W E E K

•

12

We become what we think about. Choose your thoughts wisely.

Goals:

....

....

....

....

....

Measurements:

.... Chest   Waist ....

.... Umbilicus   Hips ....

.... Right Bicep   Left Bicep ....

.... Right Thigh   Left Thigh ....

.... Right Calf   Left Calf ....

.... Weight   Body Fat ....

Progress Picture: []

This weeks Inspiration:

....

....

....

....

....

. Training Schedule .

Monday:

am ....

pm ....

Tuesday:

am ....

pm ....

Wednesday:

am ....

pm ....

Thursday:

am ....

pm ....

Friday:

am ....

pm ....

Saturday:

am ....

pm ....

Sunday

am ....

pm ....

. APPRECIATION .

.1...

.2...

.3...

W
E

.FOOD.

Meal 1:

E

....

K

....calories: ....

Meal 2:

•

....

1

....calories: ....

Meal 3:

M

....

T

....calories: ....

Meal 4:

W

....

T

....calories: ....

F

Meal 5:

S

....

S

....calories: ....

Meal 6:

....

....calories: ....

....total calories: ....

. W E I G H T • T R A I N I N G .

exercise	set 1	set 2	set 3	set 4	set 5	set 6
......	...... /	...... /	...... /	...... /	...... /	...... / ......
......	...... /	...... /	...... /	...... /	...... /	...... / ......
......	...... /	...... /	...... /	...... /	...... /	...... / ......
......	...... /	...... /	...... /	...... /	...... /	...... / ......
......	...... /	...... /	...... /	...... /	...... /	...... / ......
......	...... /	...... /	...... /	...... /	...... /	...... / ......
......	...... /	...... /	...... /	...... /	...... /	...... / ......
......	...... /	...... /	...... /	...... /	...... /	...... / ......
......	...... /	...... /	...... /	...... /	...... /	...... / ......
......	...... /	...... /	...... /	...... /	...... /	...... / ......

. A E R O B I C .

activity .... duration .... distance .... resistance .... calories

....
....
....

. R E C O V E R Y / S T R E T C H E S .

activity .... duration

....
....
....
....
....

. W A T E R .

. APPRECIATION .

.1...
.2...
.3...

W
E
E
K
•
1

M
T
W
T
F
S
S

.FOOD.

Meal 1:
....
....calories: ....

Meal 2:
....
....calories: ....

Meal 3:
....
....calories: ....

Meal 4:
....
....calories: ....

Meal 5:
....
....calories: ....

Meal 6:
....
....calories: ....
....total calories: ....

. W E I G H T • T R A I N I N G .

exercise	set 1	set 2	set 3	set 4	set 5	set 6
....	...... /	...... /	...... /	...... /	...... /	...... / ......
....	...... /	...... /	...... /	...... /	...... /	...... / ......
....	...... /	...... /	...... /	...... /	...... /	...... / ......
....	...... /	...... /	...... /	...... /	...... /	...... / ......
....	...... /	...... /	...... /	...... /	...... /	...... / ......
....	...... /	...... /	...... /	...... /	...... /	...... / ......
....	...... /	...... /	...... /	...... /	...... /	...... / ......
....	...... /	...... /	...... /	...... /	...... /	...... / ......
....	...... /	...... /	...... /	...... /	...... /	...... / ......
....	...... /	...... /	...... /	...... /	...... /	...... / ......

. A E R O B I C .

activity .... duration .... distance .... resistance .... calories

....

....

....

. R E C O V E R Y / S T R E T C H E S .

activity .... duration

....

....

....

....

....

. W A T E R .

. APPRECIATION .

.1..

.2..

.3..

W
E
E
K
.
1

M
T
W
T
F
S
S

. FOOD .

Meal 1:

....

....calories: ....

Meal 2:

....

....calories: ....

Meal 3:

....

....calories: ....

Meal 4:

....

....calories: ....

Meal 5:

....

....calories: ....

Meal 6:

....

....calories: ....

....total calories: ....

.WEIGHT•TRAINING.

exercise	set 1	set 2	set 3	set 4	set 5	set 6
....	...... /	...... /	...... /	...... /	...... /	...... / ......
....	...... /	...... /	...... /	...... /	...... /	...... / ......
....	...... /	...... /	...... /	...... /	...... /	...... / ......
....	...... /	...... /	...... /	...... /	...... /	...... / ......
....	...... /	...... /	...... /	...... /	...... /	...... / ......
....	...... /	...... /	...... /	...... /	...... /	...... / ......
....	...... /	...... /	...... /	...... /	...... /	...... / ......
....	...... /	...... /	...... /	...... /	...... /	...... / ......
....	...... /	...... /	...... /	...... /	...... /	...... / ......
....	...... /	...... /	...... /	...... /	...... /	...... / ......

.AEROBIC.

activity .... duration .... distance .... resistance .... calories

....

....

....

.RECOVERY/STRETCHES.

activity .... duration

....

....

....

....

....

.WATER.

. APPRECIATION .

.1...

.2...

.3...

W
E
E
K
·
1

M
T
W
T
F
S
S

. F O O D .

Meal 1:

....

....calories: ....

Meal 2:

....

....calories: ....

Meal 3:

....

....calories: ....

Meal 4:

....

....calories: ....

Meal 5:

....

....calories: ....

Meal 6:

....

....calories: ....

....total calories: ....

.WEIGHT•TRAINING.

exercise ...... set 1 ...... set 2 ...... set 3 ...... set 4 ...... set 5 ...... set 6

.... / .... / .... / .... / .... / .... / ......

.... / .... / .... / .... / .... / .... / ......

.... / .... / .... / .... / .... / .... / ......

.... / .... / .... / .... / .... / .... / ......

.... / .... / .... / .... / .... / .... / ......

.... / .... / .... / .... / .... / .... / ......

.... / .... / .... / .... / .... / .... / ......

.... / .... / .... / .... / .... / .... / ......

.... / .... / .... / .... / .... / .... / ......

.... / .... / .... / .... / .... / .... / ......

.AEROBIC.

activity .... duration .... distance .... resistance .... calories

....

....

....

.RECOVERY/STRETCHES.

activity .... duration

....

....

....

....

....

.WATER.

. APPRECIATION .

.1..

.2..

.3..

W
E
E
K
•
1

M
T
W
T
F
S
S

. F O O D .

Meal 1:

....

....calories: ....

Meal 2:

....

....calories: ....

Meal 3:

....

....calories: ....

Meal 4:

....

....calories: ....

Meal 5:

....

....calories: ....

Meal 6:

....

....calories: ....

....total calories: ....

.WEIGHT•TRAINING.

exercise	set 1	set 2	set 3	set 4	set 5	set 6
....	...... /	...... /	...... /	...... /	...... /	...... / ......
....	...... /	...... /	...... /	...... /	...... /	...... / ......
....	...... /	...... /	...... /	...... /	...... /	...... / ......
....	...... /	...... /	...... /	...... /	...... /	...... / ......
....	...... /	...... /	...... /	...... /	...... /	...... / ......
....	...... /	...... /	...... /	...... /	...... /	...... / ......
....	...... /	...... /	...... /	...... /	...... /	...... / ......
....	...... /	...... /	...... /	...... /	...... /	...... / ......
....	...... /	...... /	...... /	...... /	...... /	...... / ......
....	...... /	...... /	...... /	...... /	...... /	...... / ......

.AEROBIC.

activity .... duration .... distance .... resistance .... calories

....

....

....

.RECOVERY/STRETCHES.

activity .... duration

....

....

....

....

....

.WATER.

. APPRECIATION .

.1..

.2..

.3..

W
E
E
K

•

1

M
T
W
T
F
S
S

.FOOD.

Meal 1:

....

....calories: ....

Meal 2:

....

....calories: ....

Meal 3:

....

....calories: ....

Meal 4:

....

....calories: ....

Meal 5:

....

....calories: ....

Meal 6:

....

....calories: ....

....total calories: ....

. W E I G H T • T R A I N I N G.

exercise ...... set 1 ...... set 2 ...... set 3 ...... set 4 ...... set 5 ...... set 6

.... / .... / .... / .... / .... / .... / ......

.... / .... / .... / .... / .... / .... / ......

.... / .... / .... / .... / .... / .... / ......

.... / .... / .... / .... / .... / .... / ......

.... / .... / .... / .... / .... / .... / ......

.... / .... / .... / .... / .... / .... / ......

.... / .... / .... / .... / .... / .... / ......

.... / .... / .... / .... / .... / .... / ......

.... / .... / .... / .... / .... / .... / ......

.... / .... / .... / .... / .... / .... / ......

. A E R O B I C.

activity .... duration .... distance .... resistance .... calories

....

....

....

. R E C O V E R Y / S T R E T C H E S.

activity .... duration

....

....

....

....

....

. W A T E R.

. APPRECIATION .

.1..

.2..

.3..

W
E
E
K

•

1

M
T
W
T
F
S
S

. FOOD .

Meal 1:

....

....calories: ....

Meal 2:

....

....calories: ....

Meal 3:

....

....calories: ....

Meal 4:

....

....calories: ....

Meal 5:

....

....calories: ....

Meal 6:

....

....calories: ....

....total calories: ....

. W E I G H T • T R A I N I N G.

exercise	set 1	set 2	set 3	set 4	set 5	set 6
......	...... /	...... /	...... /	...... /	...... /	...... / ......
......	...... /	...... /	...... /	...... /	...... /	...... / ......
......	...... /	...... /	...... /	...... /	...... /	...... / ......
......	...... /	...... /	...... /	...... /	...... /	...... / ......
......	...... /	...... /	...... /	...... /	...... /	...... / ......
......	...... /	...... /	...... /	...... /	...... /	...... / ......
......	...... /	...... /	...... /	...... /	...... /	...... / ......
......	...... /	...... /	...... /	...... /	...... /	...... / ......
......	...... /	...... /	...... /	...... /	...... /	...... / ......
......	...... /	...... /	...... /	...... /	...... /	...... / ......

. A E R O B I C .

activity .... duration .... distance .... resistance .... calories

....

....

....

. R E C O V E R Y / S T R E T C H E S .

activity .... duration

....

....

....

....

....

. W A T E R .

CONGRATULATIONS!

.NOTES.

.NOTES.

.NOTES.

.NOTES.